THE JEWISH JESUS

How Jewish was Jesus, and what does that mean for His followers today? How does this Jewish Jesus connect with the modern State of Israel? And what happens when you read the New Testament through its original, first-century Jewish lens? All these questions are answered in this easy-to-read, clearly written, and scripturally-based book by David Hoffbrand, as the author takes you on a personal, life-changing journey of discovery. As you read these pages, your perspective will be changed.

Dr. Michael L. Brown,
bestselling author of *The Real Kosher Jesus*

In this work, David Hoffbrand has done a wonderful job in addressing the Jewishness of Jesus, the truth about Israel, and the implications for the Church. Our pastor started Gateway Church with the conviction that the Gospel is "to the Jew first." This is reflected in our first service, our first fruits giving, and our outreach priorities. We believe God's blessing upon Gateway Church has come from our commitment "to the Jew first." This rich resource will help you understand these important truths in a day when anti-Israel sentiment is on the rise.

Wayne Wilks Jr., PhD
Executive Pastor, Gateway Church, Southlake, Texas,
President Emeritus, Messianic Jewish Bible Institute,
Dallas, Texas

David takes us back to the Jewish roots of Christianity and gives a much needed biblical understanding of the importance of the Jewishness of Jesus, the centrality of Israel in God's plan and purpose and what this means for the church today. Making profound truths simple, he writes with honesty, courage and a great sense of humour, showing how these come together in an understandable and undeniable way. As you read, may you have revelation that changes your thinking, heart, life and church as it has ours!

CLIVE & JANE URQUHART
Senior Pastors, Kingdom Faith Church, Horsham, UK

As a Jewish believer in Jesus I get asked a lot, 'What part does Israel and the Jew play in God's plan for the world?' It normally evolves into a long discussion. I am happy that I can now give a very short answer: 'Read David Hoffbrand's book on the Jewishness of Jesus and you will get insight into ancient Jewish wisdom and God's true heart for the Jew.'

JEFF LESTZ
Stewardship Pastor, Hillsong UK

There are few books as clear, simple and profound in the way that *The Jewish Jesus* is. It is a significant contribution to the literature that seeks to restore an original context of meaning for interpreting the Bible that preserves the election of the Jewish people in God's plan, while affirming the Church in its role with the Jewish people. It is accessible and can be understood well by most readers. We trust that it will have a great impact.

DAN JUSTER
Founding Director,
Tikkun International Ministries, Jerusalem

David Hoffbrand introduces us to the real Jesus—the Jewish Jesus. His style will keep this book next to your night table until you finish! And if this information is new to you, I doubt you'll even put the book down.

Ron Cantor
GODTV Israel Regional Director
Author, *Identity Theft: How Jesus was Robbed of His Jewishness*

David Hoffbrand has a gift. It's a gift to bring down walls between people, movements and "stuck in the mud" attitudes. There are few people who create such an atmosphere of acceptance and celebration. David knows God. He emits this unseen grace and jumps the boundaries of his family roots and tribe with effortless strides. This book gives the understanding that has created this. It will widen your vision and create a breadth of grace that will somehow change your world.

Dave Gilpin
Senior Pastor, Hope City Church, UK

There is a widespread misunderstanding today that goes along the lines of "The church has replaced Israel and therefore God no longer sees this nation and His own special people." David Hoffbrand brings much clarity and understanding around this serious issue, using powerful biblical truths fused with brilliant wit and analogy. God's love for Israel has not diminished with the birth of the church and still holds a powerful place in the prophetic plan for all nations! You are going to love reading this book and find yourself invigorated by the truths revealed within. I feel honored to say that David is not only one of my personal friends, but he is also a pastor, leader, speaker, accomplished musician and recording artist, so you can imagine my delight in playing a small part in encouraging him to write this magnificent book!

JURGEN MATTHESIUS
Senior Pastor, C3, San Diego, USA

Through *The Jewish Jesus*, David Hoffbrand articulately unpacks centuries of church tradition and, through the lens of desiring to see a healthy church, rewires the reader's thinking. This causes a significant and essential realignment of our mindset regarding Jewish and Gentile believers. A highly recommended read for people who have a desire to go deeper in their relationship with Jesus - it's a fresh focus on who He really is.

ROSS ABRAHAM
Senior Pastor, Elevation Church, Goldcoast, Australia
Oceania Chairman, International Network of Churches

David has an incredible ability to bring alive the New Testament in its original context, in a way that brings clarity and understanding. This has been a tremendous help in teaching people to know Jesus, and in building our church to be one that carries the heart of God. I believe this book is going to have a massive impact on the wider church's understanding in these areas!

DAVID HARLAND
Senior Pastor, CityCoast Church, Brighton, UK

THE JEWISH JESUS

RECONNECTING WITH THE TRUTH ABOUT JESUS, ISRAEL, & THE CHURCH

DAVID HOFFBRAND

DESTINY IMAGE® PUBLISHERS, INC.
P.O. Box 310, Shippensburg, PA 17257-0310
"Promoting Inspired Lives."

This book and all other Destiny Image and Destiny Image Fiction books are available at Christian bookstores and distributors worldwide.

Cover design by Ian Barnard
Interior design by Terry Clifton

For more information on foreign distributors, call 717-532-3040.
Reach us on the Internet: www.destinyimage.com.

ISBN 13 TP: 978-0-7684-1104-1
ISBN 13 eBook: 978-0-7684-1105-8
ISBN 13 HC: 978-0-7684-1532-2
ISBN 13 LP: 978-0-7684-1533-9

For Worldwide Distribution, Printed in the U.S.A.

1 2 3 4 5 6 7 8 / 21 20 19 18 17

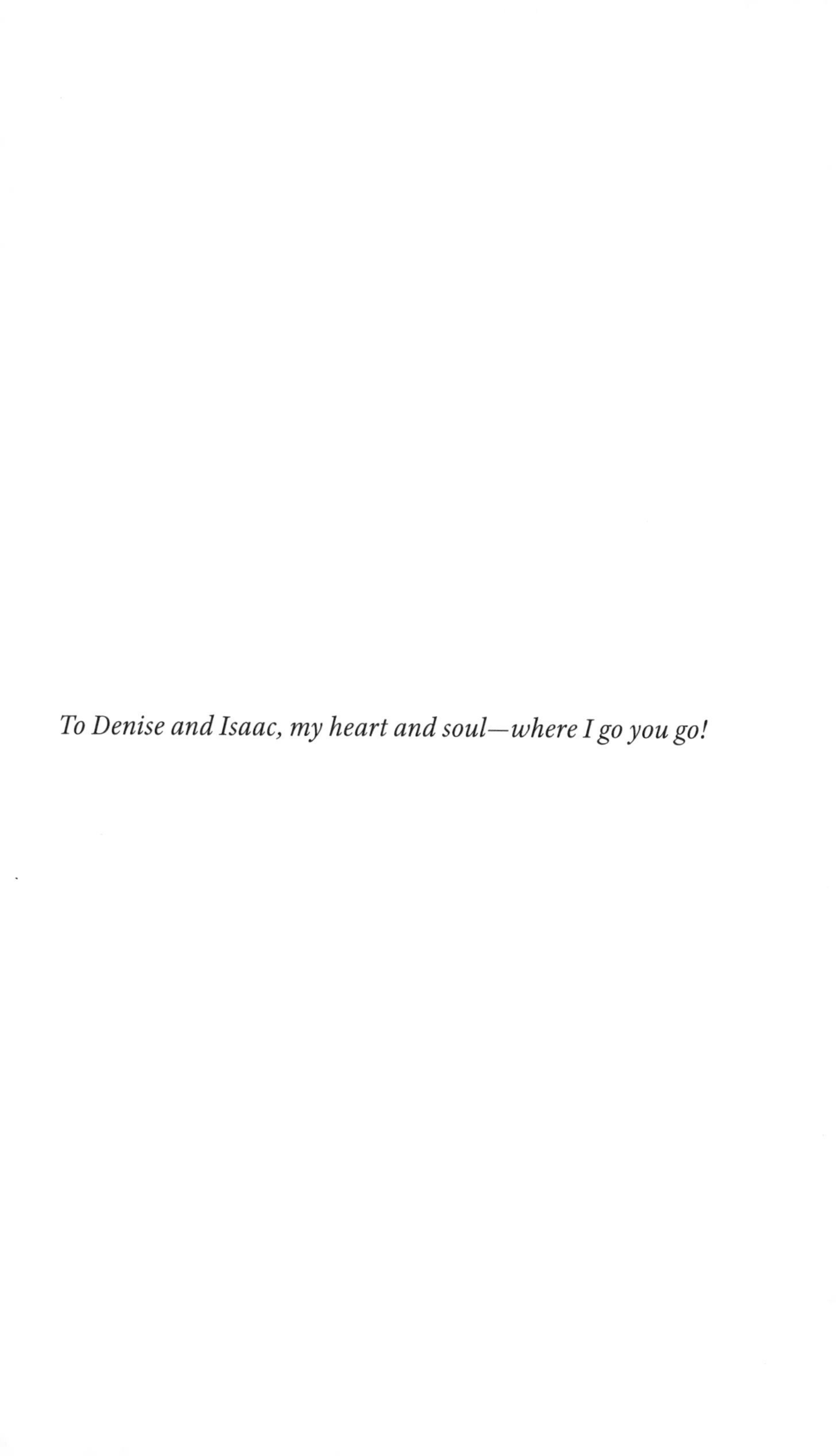

To Denise and Isaac, my heart and soul—where I go you go!

CONTENTS

Introduction

Have you ever been for a sight test? I've had pretty good eyesight for most of my life. Recently though, it's been a struggle to see details clearly, and I began to wonder if something had changed, so I booked a sight test.

The lady set my chin in the device and got me to look at the rows of letters and, sure enough, I could see the huge letters at the top and a few lines below them, but underneath that there were just rows of little dark blobs. I'm sure many of you will have had the same experience, but it was new for me.

Then she slotted some lenses into place and—bam! There were all these rows of letters in glorious focus. It was like now I could see the details, whereas before, all I could see were the headlines.

I think sometimes this is how it can feel when we read the Bible and think about Jesus. We see the headlines—the key truths—yet it feels like so much of the picture is blurred.

We've all had the experience of wondering what certain passages in the Bible mean, wondering what Jesus meant when He said this or that, and giving up, thinking, "I just can't see it."

The trouble is, the Bible only comes alive in us as we understand it, as the truth sets us free.

Like the letters on those lower rows, however, the detail is right there, hidden in plain sight, and God wants us to move beyond the headlines so we can know Jesus more intimately.

I believe that the key to this is to *look at the Bible in its original Jewish context*. When we do this, it is like putting on the right lenses—suddenly all those missing details reappear. Our picture of Jesus becomes clearer than ever before!

Over the last fifty years or so especially, there has been much research revealing the Jewishness of Jesus, and scholars such as Dwight Pryor have shown us how putting on 'Hebraic spectacles' can help us to see a more accurate and detailed picture of who He is.[1]

Actually, before we can put on new lenses, we need to take the ones with the old prescription off. The truth is that over the last two thousand years every culture and era, even every individual, has painted Jesus in the light of its own needs and expectations. We all see Jesus through a filter of our traditions without realizing it.

There have been so many different versions of Jesus—Social Justice Jesus! Freedom Fighter Jesus! Hippie Jesus! Mystic Teacher Jesus! So many old lenses that affect the way we see Him.

Now imagine the clarity you would have, the level of intimacy you would experience, if you had the perfect, tailor-made prescription for you—the lens that allows you to see the authentic, original Jesus, and the one upon which all the others are based.

That's the *Jewish Jesus.* I want to introduce you to Him—the Jesus of the Bible—in a way you perhaps haven't experienced before, because if knowing Jesus is our goal then surely we want to see the details, not just the headlines?

You see, the one Jesus who is most clearly in the Bible, the one who ties together all of the rest and yet seems most missing today for us, is the Jewish Jesus. He is Jesus the healer. He is Jesus the Savior. He is the head of the church and the one we're following.

In this book, I want us to look beyond our traditional thinking. We will find that so much more detail emerges as we restore the lens of the Jewish context in which Jesus and His followers actually lived and taught.

As the subtitle suggests, the book is divided into three sections:

1. Reconnecting with the Jewish Jesus
2. The truth about Israel
3. Implications for the church

These flow naturally from each other—as we reconnect with the Jewish Jesus, it causes us to re-examine God's purposes for the Jewish people and to consider what the Bible really says about Israel.

This in turn leads us to ask the question—what is the relevance of all this for the church today? How can we incorporate it in a way that enriches our lives as individuals and church communities?

When I was first exploring these issues, I thought it was going to be a complex process. Instead of something mystical, however, I felt God say to me that the key is simple—read without religion. In case I struggled with that, I could boil it down to this acronym: REWIRE (Read Without Religion).

God impressed on me that all we need to do is read the Bible as if we hadn't read it before—to remove the lens of our traditions, which causes us to skip past so many passages without seeing the details.

This is not about trying to live according to a Jewish culture you never even knew, but it is about properly understanding the Bible and God's heart. It is about a return to the Jewish mindset that is at the heart of the Christian message and writings.

I truly believe that as we go on this journey together the details that were there all along will come into focus, and we will know Jesus like we never have before.

NOTE

1. Dwight Pryor, *Behold the Man* (Dayton, Ohio: Centre for Judaic Christian Studies, 2005), 13. This is from the companion study textbook to the DVD teaching series, Session 9. www.jcstudies.com.

PART ONE

RECONNECTING WITH THE JEWISH JESUS

Who Is Jesus?

I grew up in a very typical Jewish family. We went to synagogue on the religious holidays, but not by any means every week. We celebrated Chanukah rather than Christmas, Passover rather than Easter, and also the other Jewish festivals outlined in the Bible. We ate all the traditional foods associated with those festivals and Jewish life generally (if you've been to a Jewish deli you may understand a bit of where I'm coming from here).

My great-grandparents had all come to England around the turn of the century, when a great deal of persecution of the Jews was taking place in mainland Europe, in what was then the Russian Empire.

On my father's side, they settled in Bradford, in the north of England. My paternal grandfather, who died before I was born, was a tailor. There's a Jewish cemetery in Bradford where most of this side of the family are buried (I'm particularly fond of "Wolf Hoffbrand"—the original Jewish X-Man).

On my mother's side, they settled in the East End of London, where my other grandfather was also in the "rag trade." To his dying day, he seemed unable to walk past me if I was wearing a new suit without grabbing the lapel and proclaiming it "a nice bit of *schmutter.*"[1]

A lot of my parents' friends, as well as my own, were Jewish. This meant there were *bar mitzvahs* and *bat mitzvahs*[2] (for boys and girls respectively) at regular intervals, either for a relative or for someone's son or daughter.

I had my bar mitzvah at 13, as all Jewish boys do. For months I learned the portion of the Torah (Old Testament) to be sung in synagogue on the day in question. Once I had taken this active role in the service, I would be considered a man in the community, no longer a boy (*bar mitzvah* means, literally, 'son of the commandment', and describes the idea that the individual now becomes morally and legally responsible for their actions and for following God's commandments).

The day finally arrived, and I just about carried it off. At the beginning of my part of the service, I looked down to find that the blessings I was supposed to start with were nowhere to be found. I panicked. Where was the page with them on?! There followed a muttered dispute between my teacher and I about whether I knew the blessings or not, while several hundred people sat wondering what was going on—a terrifying comedy moment that no 13-year-old wants to experience! After that, I was *a man!* That evening, as is typical, we finished with an enormous party hosted by my parents.

In truth, I more or less stopped going to synagogue after that. I didn't have a sense of faith or of knowing God, and had little interest in organized religion. As many Jewish people do, I maintained a sense of my identity and background, albeit somewhat distantly, but there was no sense for me of connecting this to faith in God.

On the inside, however, I had a spiritual yearning—a desire to know the truth. For many years I searched for a path toward "enlightenment" and inner truth, looking in all manner of places. From Buddhism to magic, from meditation to the I Ching—you name it, I looked there!

The very last thing I wanted to be was a *Christian.* I saw this as the ultimate betrayal, the furthest step I could take away from being a Jew—even the very abandonment of my Jewish identity. Other things felt weird, but only Christianity felt abhorrent.

This is a sentiment common to many, if not most, Jewish people I know. By the end of this book, hopefully the reasons (and some of the remedy) for this will be clearer, but I believe that there are two key underlying reasons—first, the misrepresentation of Jesus by the church over the centuries; and second, the persecution of Jewish people by the church over the same period. The first made way for the second.

The church has presented Jesus with so little of His Jewish context or identity, as we shall see, that no Jewish person really recognizes Him as their own without a struggle. In fact, the church has generally so disassociated itself from the Jewish aspects of who Jesus is and of His teaching and mission that He is often presented for all intents and purposes as a Gentile (non-Jewish) man.

Furthermore, the reality is that no organization has been so directly responsible for persecution of Jewish people over the centuries as the church, and even Christian society generally. Many Christians today are unaware of this.

We will revisit this in more depth later, but to summarize, the church has often accused the Jewish people of being "Christ killers," and the source of all kinds of evil in this world. At different times and in different places, Jewish communities have been threatened with "conversion" to Christianity on pain of death and expelled time and again from supposedly Christian societies. And this has all been done in the name of the Jewish Savior Himself!

While many of the extreme and often bizarre assertions regarding the Jewish people linger in certain circles and so emerge from these sources today—for instance, from radical Islamist preachers and far-right extremist groups—they almost all found expression initially through the mainstream church. This continued over the centuries, affecting Jewish people wherever they settled in the western world. Therefore, when a Jewish person hears the name "Jesus," the associations they make are completely different from what you might expect and are usually very negative rather than even neutral.

So when God began to reach out to me and show me that Jesus was who He said He was and the answer I had been looking for, I stalled, worried, prevaricated, and pushed God away, appalled at the enormity and finality of this conclusion. *Was I to cut away the last vestiges of my Jewishness to follow this Christian God*?

It took a series of amazing supernatural experiences, over several years, for me to acknowledge that God was real and, more so, that Jesus did indeed seem to be who He said He was.

Even then, I avoided being part of a church or calling myself a follower of Jesus, until God clearly demonstrated to me that Jesus and the church went hand in hand.

And yet...and yet, *Jesus and His disciples who formed the early church were all Jewish.* Accepting Him was not the farthest but the very *closest* step I could take away from the Judaism I had grown up with. What we call "Christianity" grew out of the Jewish faith and could never have existed without it.

Moreover, its core remains Jewish—so much more so than we realize, as we will discover. *Jesus Himself never used the words "Christian" or "Christianity" but exclusively taught and spoke in Jewish terms.*

Most Jewish people I know who have embraced Jesus as their Messiah have been through a similar agonizing process, often involving very supernatural and overwhelming experiences, as though God were compensating for these extra hurdles that He has to overcome.

Where then did this sense of abandoning my Jewishness come from?

It is true that many of the Jewish religious leaders, and ultimately Judaism in general, rejected and still reject the claims of Jesus to be the Messiah promised to Israel (even though many Jewish people *did* accept Him).

However, what is also true is that the church has so lost and abandoned its Jewish roots, that it has lost all sense of the Jewishness of Jesus and His teaching, and of the Bible itself. In fact, it has actually lost touch with the Jewish roots and context of much of what it believes and practices.

Most believers are unaware of this, leaving them and the church the poorer for it. How often do we stop to consider, for instance, that much of the Bible we read is a translation of a translation? The Gospels we read in English are translated from a Greek text that was itself a translation from Hebrew sources. They describe the teachings of a man who spoke Hebrew and Aramaic, not Greek.

You could attend many churches for every service of the year and hear almost nothing that would tell you Jesus was Jewish. Is this not a little odd?

In fact, it is not only that the church has *lost touch* with its Jewish roots over the centuries, at various times there has also been a very deliberate and active cutting away of all things Jewish from the church, its understanding, and its practices. And although most of us are not aware of this process, *we still live with its legacy.*

That legacy has caused a terrible loss to the church and has done a great disservice to us as followers of Jesus.

I firmly believe that when we recover this aspect of our faith we will also recover much of what we are seeking for our lives personally and in the church today. At the same time, we will get rid of much of what turns non-Christians off the message we are trying to deliver to them.

Too often they see people who make converts through one prayer and ignore the hypocrisies of a lifestyle without discipleship. People who proclaim they follow faithfully the teachings in a book they barely study or read, much less understand. People who claim to be part of a revolutionary movement, yet have often seemed to reduce it to attending a building once a week. People who claim to follow a loving God, yet define themselves by what they avoid for fear of contamination rather than by the true inner transformation and walk of faith that shows people God's love.

When we restore the Jewish roots, we restore the foundations of discipleship, true study of the Bible, a transformed lifestyle (not just a different set of beliefs), true community, and much more, as we will see. These are all inherent in the Jewish mindset and the framework within which Jesus and His early disciples operated.

I am not saying that these things are entirely missing in the church. Of course not. Simply that there is a richness of detail and context that we can recover when we restore the Jewish lens.

Fundamentally, we will learn to know, present, and represent Jesus more accurately as individuals and as a body. This is surely the aspiration of every follower of Jesus, for themselves and for His church.

I also believe something else—that when we present an accurate picture of Jesus and His body, the church, we will enable more Jewish people to discover an appreciation for this greatest of Jews, and re-examine His claims to be their Messiah.

NOTES

1. *Schmutter* is a Yiddish word meaning "clothes." Yiddish is a mixture of German and Hebrew, spoken by a large number of Jews before the Holocaust, and still by some today. Like many Jews from their generation, both my grandparents spoke English sprinkled with Yiddish words for color.

2. A bar/bat mitzvah is the Jewish coming of age, where a boy or girl becomes a fully fledged member of the community, and it is the origin of the Christian confirmation tradition.

CHAPTER 2

JESUS THE MAN

The psychiatrist R.D. Laing was so famous for his theories on mental illness and identity that in the 1960s and '70s he was almost like a rock star. He told a story about how, years later, someone came up to him in the street and asked him, "Excuse me, did you used to be R.D. Laing?" As someone who taught about identity, this seemed poignant to him.

I think that as Christians we can have a similar sense of confusion about Jesus, as if He had a split personality and we were asking Him, "Excuse me, did You used to be the Jewish Jesus?"

When we say, "Oh, yes, Jesus was Jewish," I think in our minds what we really mean is that He went through a Jewish *phase,* like Picasso went through his "blue period" where his paintings tended to have blue as the predominate color.

The sense is that Picasso passed *through* this period on his journey to becoming a great artist. I think the picture that most of us have in our minds is that Jesus passed through His period of being Jewish on His way to becoming the Messiah. As if He grew out of it, like an awkward teenage phase.

Often, as Christians, we seem to have no sense that the Jewishness of Jesus is in any way a fundamental aspect of who He is—certainly not now, even though we will confidently proclaim that "He is the same yesterday, today, and forever!"

It's as if Jesus dropped out of heaven into a Jewish body and culture, undercover, and gave the Jewish people of the day an opportunity to join a completely different religion called Christianity, with an entirely different set of values, principles, and traditions from their own. Then He dropped the mic and left them to figure it out.

Sadly, the story goes, those Jews completely misunderstood what He was saying and all rejected Him, preferring to stay in their own religion. So, instead, He took His wares elsewhere.

If this is the picture that you have in your mind, I hope you will start to see just how misleading it is.

I saw a TV program a few years back about a very old Byzantine church. There was a fresco on the wall—a picture of Jesus. He looked blond, blue-eyed—very much the European man!

However, they found that underneath was an older painting of Jesus, and underneath that another, even older, and so on, back to the earliest days of the building (from around AD 600) in the Byzantine era.

The interesting thing was, the older the picture uncovered, the more like a typical Jewish man Jesus looked, with dark brown hair, brown eyes, and olive skin.

I believe this is a perfect analogy for what God wants to do in our minds and the church—strip away the layers that have been put on Jesus through the centuries so we can see Him as He really is.

We have a great picture of this when we look at the life of Joseph in the book of Genesis. Joseph was the son favored by his father, and he told his brothers that God had showed him in a dream that he would rule over them all. In their jealousy, his brothers planned to betray and kill Joseph, but through the intervention of his older brother he was sold into slavery instead.

He was thrown into prison after being falsely accused, yet through God's amazing plan he was plucked out of prison to become the second-in-command of Egypt, sitting at Pharaoh's right hand. Because of this, he was able to rescue Egypt and the surrounding nations from starvation and death in the famine that came afterward.

Joseph was given a new name and a new set of Egyptian clothes. He looked so different, in fact, that when his brothers were forced to seek help in Egypt during the famine and came before him, they didn't recognize him.

He knew *them*, however, and longed to reveal his true heart to them because, in spite of everything, he still loved them. Finally, he revealed himself to them through all those layers of foreign clothing, and they saw their brother for who he was! They understood how he loved them, and so did all those around him in the court of Pharaoh. The Egyptians saw their savior in a new light.

This is an amazing picture of Jesus: rejected by His brothers, sent to prison, yet resurrected from death to sit at the right hand of the Father. Jesus also became the Savior of a whole multitude of people from different nations, who were not originally His own people. He too has been given a new name and dressed in the clothes of the cultures who adopted Him as their Lord.

Yet underneath, He remains the *Jewish* Messiah, ready for the layers to be stripped away so that He can fully reveal Himself to both Jew and Gentile.

Joseph said to his brothers, "Please, come closer." In other words, "Look more closely and you'll see beneath these layers that it's really me, your brother!" So this is the *invitation*—to come closer and look beneath the layers of tradition, to see the Jewish Jesus and hear His heart for His brothers, His original family.

The invitation is still there for His Jewish brothers and sisters, but also for everyone who is willing, to see Him and know Him as He really is, behind the Gentile clothes and the Gentile name.

The Bible even says that Joseph had a new Gentile, Egyptian bride called Asenath, given to him by Pharaoh. This is a picture of the church as we see it now. Through her, Joseph had two sons, Ephraim and Manasseh, who, although initially Egyptian, eventually had their Jewish identities restored just as Joseph did.

To me, this paints an incredible picture for us of how God wants us all—believers who are children through the seemingly Gentile church—to understand and embrace our true inheritance.

The current occupants of that Byzantine building didn't have any idea they were looking at a changed picture—one that covered up the older, more accurate picture. I think it's the same for us. We've inherited this revised picture of Jesus and so we don't really question it. We need to uncover the original and true representation, because if we want to know, present, and *represent* Jesus properly, it's vital that our picture of Him is accurate.

We must understand that, like the picture, it is not a question of *adding* a layer of Jewish culture but of *uncovering* a truer representation of Jesus. This is a fundamental principle because so often people's anxiety in starting down this path is that they feel they will *lose* Jesus. I believe the opposite is true—we will know Him more as He really is and learn to understand and love Him more deeply. It will only enrich our faith and enlighten us further.

It's natural that each culture paints Jesus to some extent in the light they want to see Him, which is often related to the needs of a particular time. The Jews at the time of His coming wanted to paint Him as a revolutionary fighter who would overthrow their Roman conquerors. Ever since, people have been trying to paint Jesus in a light that would best suit their needs.

This process leads to serious problems, however. If I want to get to know a famous person and think they're English when in fact they're French, then all sorts of misunderstandings may arise. I'll make assumptions that are incorrect and misleading. I will misunderstand the context of their thoughts and ideas and the idioms, images, and symbolism they use. I will misinterpret their references. These misinterpretations will reverberate through everything I say to others about this person.

In the same way, if our faith comes from our relationship with Jesus, then a correct understanding of who we're following and of His teaching is surely the most important thing we can develop.

Often, people fear that looking into this will create a burden—another set of dos and don'ts we have to adopt. Sometimes, people have been put off even looking at this by ministries or people who make them feel as if they have to become Jewish or as if they have to start waving flags and dancing in circles in special ways!

Let me reassure you, *that's not what this is about.* First, I'm Jewish and I don't have an inclination to do any of those things. (If you do, feel free. I'm not judging, just stating a preference.)

Second, as we shall see, even if any of those things had anything to do with it, *Jews are supposed to be Jews, and Gentiles, Gentiles!* If you're a Gentile, you don't need to be circumcised, and you don't have to behave as if you're Jewish, either. (I can't think of an equally simple analogy for women, so apologies. Please take the gist!)

Jesus said in Mark 7:13 that the traditions of the Pharisees made the Word of God of no effect in their lives. Our traditions can do the same. They can be like a lens that colors our perceptions. So this is about taking *off* that lens.

This is what God was speaking about to me when He told me the key was simply "REWIRE"—"Read Without Religion."

We're not aiming to read things *into* the Bible that are not there or are obscure, but to get *out* what is already there so we can understand the true meaning of what we are reading. That is what restoring the Jewish context is all about.

With this in mind, let's take a look at the life and ministry of Jesus.

JESUS THE JEW

What is the very first thing we read in the New Testament about Jesus? Matthew 1:1 says that He is "the Son of David, the Son of Abraham." Why Abraham? Why David?

The writer is saying clearly that Jesus is the fulfillment of the promises made to Abraham, the Jewish patriarch, and to David the Jewish king—promises that, through Abraham, all nations of the earth would be blessed, promises to David that a descendant of his would be on the throne of Israel forever.

What was said about Jesus before His birth? In Matthew 1:21, the angel says, "And you shall call His name Jesus, for He will save *His* people from their sins."

The name *Jesus* is simply a translation of the Hebrew name *Yeshua*, which means "the Lord saves." The word *Christ* is from a Greek translation of the Jewish word *Maschiach*, from which we get our word *Messiah*. Christ is not Jesus' surname, but a translation of His Jewish title.

In Matthew 2:6, the priests and religious leaders quote the prophet Micah to explain that the Messiah will be born in Bethlehem and be "the shepherd for my people Israel" (NLT), and in Luke 1:32-33, the angel declares of Jesus, "The Lord God will give him the throne of his ancestor David. And he will reign over Israel [or *the house of Jacob*, another name for Israel] forever; his Kingdom will never end" (NLT).

So if Jesus is no longer reigning over Israel, the angel got it wrong!

What did the early disciples say when they found Jesus? In John 1:41 and 45, Andrew and Philip proclaim, "We have found the Messiah...the very person Moses and the prophets wrote about!" (NLT).

Jesus said of Himself that He didn't come in opposition to the Law and the prophets—what we call the "Old Testament," which is the foundation for all Jewish life.

Consider these simple but vital questions: Where did the terms *Old Testament* and *New Testament* come from from? Did God designate those two sections of the Bible this way? In reality, the roots of these terms did not even begin to emerge until 150 years or more after the death of Jesus; and it was much later, at the end of the fourth century, that the scholar Jerome translated the Greek word for "covenant" using the Latin word *testamentum*, from which we get our English word *testament*.

This is clearly misleading, because what we call the Old Testament contains much more than the Mosaic covenant and commandments God gave at Sinai, and the New Covenant was not made until the end of the Gospels.

This way of thinking about the Bible would have been completely alien to Jesus and His followers. To the Jewish people, and therefore to Jesus, the "Old Testament" consists of three sections—the Torah, the Prophets, and the Writings (summed up in Hebrew by the word *Tanakh,* an acronym using the first letters of each word). These Scriptures are the only ones the early church had and referred to always as holy, useful, "sharper than a two-edged sword," and so on.

When John starts his Gospel, "In the beginning was the Word, and the Word was with God, and the Word was God" (John 1:1), he is partly talking about Jesus as the living embodiment of the Jewish Scriptures we have called "Old." The words "in the beginning" pointed people to the opening words of Genesis 1.

If I offer you an old piece of cake or a new piece of cake, however, which would you prefer? The terms *Old Testament* and *New Testament,* seemingly so innocuous, actually create a framework that colors our whole thinking and distorts how we see everything in the Bible. I will continue to use these terms for simplicity, but one of the best ways to REWIRE our thinking and restore the Jewish lens is to begin to look past these labels.

Peter, James, and John saw an amazing confirmation of the continuity between the "Old" and "New" Testaments when Jesus took them up the mountain with Him.

> *Six days later Jesus took Peter and the two brothers, James and John, and led them up a high mountain to be alone. As the men watched, Jesus' appearance was transformed so that his*

> *face shone like the sun, and his clothes became as white as light. Suddenly, Moses and Elijah appeared and began talking with Jesus* (Matthew 17:1-3 NLT).

Moses represented the Law to the Jewish people. He was the man God used to deliver them out of Egypt, and it was through Moses that God gave Israel His commandments, the whole framework for their society.

Elijah was a great prophet who did amazing miracles in Israel. God spoke through another prophet, Malachi, about how Elijah would come again:

> *Remember to obey the Law of Moses, my servant—all the decrees and regulations that I gave him on Mount Sinai for all Israel. Look, I am sending you the prophet Elijah before the great and dreadful day of the Lord arrives* (Malachi 4:4-5 NLT).

Malachi draws a direct line between the Law of Moses, Elijah, and the coming of the Messiah, so the Jewish people expected Elijah to come in tandem with the Messiah, heralding His coming. In fact, each year at Passover, Jewish people still pour a cup of wine for Elijah, which they leave undrunk to represent the promise that Elijah is coming again to herald the Messiah.

Jesus made it clear, however, that John the Baptist was a partial fulfillment of the one whom Malachi had been prophesying about, and that He Himself was the promised Messiah. Then, in addition, Elijah himself came and stood with Jesus and Moses on the mountain.

By appearing with Jesus, Moses and Elijah affirmed that He was the fulfillment of the prophecies and promises made to the Jewish people, and reinforced the statement of Jesus that He stood *with*, not against, the Law and the prophets of Israel.

Moreover, when we look at how Jesus is presented in the book of Revelation, at the end of all time even, we see something very interesting: He *still identifies Himself by His Jewish heritage.* He is *still* called, in Revelation 5:5, "the Lion of the tribe of Judah, the Root of David," and in Revelation 22:16, "the root and the Offspring of David."

It seems that He was not passing through a Jewish phase after all. His Jewish identity will continue to have relevance even at the end—even for eternity. We neglect this at our peril. He is, as we know, *the same yesterday, today, and forever.*

We can begin to see that the Jewishness of Jesus may not be a side issue after all.

His Childhood

Jesus wasn't just *born* a Jew, though. The Bible says He was circumcised on the eighth day, as outlined in God's instructions to Moses. He then grew up in the Jewish culture.

I think when we read the Gospels and see that there is so little about the upbringing and adolescence of Jesus, we can either presume nothing happened at all, or else we imagine that in fact all sorts of exotic things were happening to which we are not privy.

We know that Jesus was 30 when He began His ministry. I think we almost assume that He was just biding His time till He could begin—a sort of spiritual twiddling of the thumbs!

This way of thinking causes us to emphasize the *deity* of Jesus. However, it places Him far away from our grasp. His humanity becomes a mere disguise. He becomes more mysterious, and living the life He has for us seems even more unattainable. *To restore the Jewishness of Jesus means in part to restore His humanity and therefore His relevance to us. It brings Him closer.*

In all probability, the reason so little is mentioned about his life before the age of 30 is that, even if Jesus Himself was unique, much of what happened through this period of His life was typical for a Jewish boy growing up in Jesus' time.

The whole rhythm of His early life would have been dictated by the Jewish religious calendar, as laid out in the Torah, because religion and culture were completely entwined. Each year He would have celebrated the biblical festivals with His family. Thirty was the age at which rabbis traditionally began their ministries, so His "late start" was not unusual either.

The Bible says that Jesus came "in the likeness of men" (Phil. 2:7) and submitted himself to those limitations. Luke 2:52 says that "Jesus grew in wisdom and in stature" (NLT) and correspondingly in favor with God and people. His understanding of His identity and mission surely developed as this process continued.

Just before Luke says this, he tells us how Jesus and His family went up to Jerusalem to celebrate the Passover festival every year (as God commanded the Israelites to). Luke recounts an incident when Jesus, aged 12, disappeared for three days.

It says in Luke 2:46 that "they found Him in the temple, sitting in the midst of the teachers, both listening to them and asking them questions." He was curious—keen to develop and test His understanding, as Jewish boys did. They were astonished by Him, because He was so young to be so wise, but He hadn't yet preached His great messages to the crowds.

Jesus was precocious. The Bible, however, makes it clear that Jesus had to grow and learn. He wasn't just hanging around till it was time for His ministry to begin. And Luke is showing us that Jesus grew *in the context of His Jewish upbringing.*

The Jewish pattern of learning for boys was something like this: from six to ten years of age they would learn the first five books of the Bible, also called the *Torah* (a word that we translate "Law," and which can also be used to refer to the whole of what we call the "Old Testament"). This stage is known as the *Bet Sefer* or "house of the book."

Jesus would have memorized the Scriptures by heart, as all Jewish boys had to—remember, the average person didn't have a copy of the Torah, so they had to know it by heart in order to discuss it.

From ten to fourteen years of age, Jewish boys would learn the rest of the Scriptures, up to Malachi, and also learn the technique of asking and answering questions regarding the interpretation of Scripture. This was known as the *Bet Talmud* or "house of learning."

Jesus would have learned about the teachings of the rabbis and how they interpreted Scripture so as to apply it to everyday life. So when He was at the Temple, he was practicing exactly that!

Finally, at around 13 or 14 years of age, the best students would choose a rabbi and ask to be his disciple. The rabbi would then vet the boy to decide if he was worthy or not to carry his "yoke," or teaching. This is what Jesus was referring to when He said, in Matthew 11:30, "My yoke is easy."

Clearly, Jesus didn't ask to be the disciple of any rabbi, presumably because He knew His Father was instructing Him personally, alongside any other input. He did ask John to baptize Him, demonstrating His submission to divine authority. However, in other respects it seems apparent that He would have received the same instruction as other Jewish boys.

He heard the arguments and controversies of the day, the interpretations of different teachers, and He experienced and saw the Jewish way of discipleship and learning. He heard the parables and stories used by the rabbis to teach and train their disciples. He heard specific techniques of instruction.

What, then, did He do when it came to teaching His own disciples? As we will see, *He applied the same principles and techniques as He had learned and seen.*

When we look through this lens, we see more of the *humanity* of Jesus and His identification with us. We see Him learning and growing into the fullness of who He was called to be as a man. In this, we recognize that we can do the same by embracing a similar process. We may never be *exactly* like Him in this life, but we can become *more and more* like Him as God works in our hearts and we too grow in "wisdom and stature."

Instead of simply waiting passively for someone else to tell us what to believe, we can learn to understand the Scriptures and to ask and answer the right kinds of questions. We can grow in maturity when we embrace this model, and the church can become healthier as a result.

Church leaders can embrace the need to create a *Bet Talmud* or house of learning, not just a house of *believing*, and the everyday followers of Jesus can embrace the need to take responsibility for their growth rather than expecting to always be spoon-fed.

I believe all of this is God's intention, rather than setting us a mysterious and unattainable goal. Jesus understood His identity, mission, and purpose by the Holy Spirit's revelation through the Word. We can do the same.

When Jesus was performing His great miracles, some Jewish people suddenly remembered what they already knew about Him. *"Wait a minute—isn't this Joseph's son?"* they asked (see Luke 4:22; John 6:42). But while they found it hard to see past His humanity to see His divinity, it feels like the church has often suffered from the opposite problem—we have focused so much on the *divinity* of Jesus that we have found it hard to see His *humanity*. Restoring the Jewish lens helps restore our vision of who Jesus is as a man.

CHAPTER 4

THE MINISTRY OF JESUS

Now that we have seen that Jesus was born and raised as a Jew, what about His ministry?

Often people think He came to the Jewish people with this new philosophy and blew apart the whole framework of Jewish thinking. Our traditions lead us to assume He came to signal the end of Judaism and the beginning of a new religion called Christianity. It is from this logic that the opposition to everything Jewish comes.

The average believer may even suppose that Jesus' life followed a traditional Jewish pattern *until His ministry.* From this point, however, we tend to think that He abandoned His Jewish roots to found Christianity.

In fact, nothing could be further from the truth. His life *and His ministry* both followed a very Jewish pattern.

It was common for Jewish boys to learn Scripture at a young age, as we have seen. It was common for rabbis, or teachers of the Torah, to also have a profession. It was, in fact, forbidden to charge for teaching the Scriptures. Rabbis could accept hospitality and voluntary support from people in return for their teaching, but no more.

We see both these patterns, for instance, in the lives of Jesus and Paul. Paul continued to make tents at times throughout his ministry, and both were supported by voluntary contributions from others.

Some people have said that Jesus must have traveled to India to learn from gurus over there, so alien do they think His teaching and methods are! This just stems from not understanding the Jewish context of Jesus' ministry.

It was common for rabbis to raise up disciples. John the Baptist had disciples. Paul says in Acts that he was a disciple of Gamaliel's, who was known to have many disciples. Jesus was doing what all rabbis did.

Just before the time of Jesus' ministry, there were two great rabbis, Hillel and Shammai, and each had many disciples. Hillel only died in AD 10. Collectively, they were known as the "house of Hillel" and the "house of Shammai," and they had many debates about the correct interpretation of God's teachings. Jesus was often asked to give His opinion on these same subjects, and He responded in a way that showed which way He sided.

One famous quote from Hillel is his response when asked to sum up the whole of God's teachings, the Torah. Hillel responded, "That which is hateful to you, do not do to your fellow. That is the whole Torah; the rest is the explanation; go and learn."[1] This saying is known as "the Golden Rule."

Jesus was once with a group of Pharisees and Sadducees, religious leaders at the time. We read in Matthew 22:35-40 that:

> *One of them, an expert in religious law, tried to trap Him with this question: "Teacher, which is the most important commandment in the law of Moses?" Jesus replied, "'You must love the Lord your God with all your heart, all your soul, and all your mind.' This is the first and greatest commandment. A second is equally important: 'Love your neighbor as yourself.' The entire law and all the demands of the prophets are based on these two commandments"* (NLT).

Isn't it striking how similar His answer is to Hillel's, who had lived just before His ministry began? Except Jesus' answer is yet more beautiful, as though He were upgrading Hillel's comment. As always, Jesus places the greatest emphasis on the positive application of God's love through our lives, rather than on what we are to avoid.

We know that Jesus taught many thousands of people and prayed for the sick and oppressed people of the region, and yet what was at the *heart* of His ministry?

He raised up 120 disciples, 12 of them close to Him, and three of them key leaders. These were the people who carried on His ministry after He left, not the thousands who followed Him or for whom He prayed. He poured His life into His closest disciples. He ate, traveled, talked, laughed, and generally "did life" with these core people.

Some of His messages may seem hard, but we must remember that we are not reading what it means to "be a

Christian" or "go to church." We are reading what it means to be a true *disciple* of Jesus in the *Jewish* sense.

Discussions of how to interpret God's commands and of how to live them out in a community were central to the Jewish understanding of how to live a life that was pleasing to God. This is sometimes referred to as the "oral traditions."

A book called the Talmud is the key text for the interpretation of the Torah in the Jewish religion. It collects together the teachings of the most important rabbis over hundreds of years. It was written down formally in AD 200 and after, but it was transmitted orally for centuries, in different forms, prior to this. This book states that it is important to raise up many disciples (Avot 1:1)!

It would come as a complete surprise to most of us that much of what Jesus said had parallels in the words of other rabbis and in the Talmud.

It was, for instance, stated in the Talmud that a disciple needed to honor his rabbi over his father or mother, and attend to the rabbi's needs before attending to those of his relatives. This again has striking parallels to what Jesus said to His disciples.

The very word *disciple* that we use is a translation of a Greek word that itself was a translation of the word *talmid*, meaning "student." Actually, that word, used by Jesus and all rabbis, has no direct equivalent in English. For a talmid seeks not simply to study and learn with his rabbi, or teacher, but *to become like him in every way.*

Our traditions focus on trying to get people to "become Christians," by which we mean to say a prayer and ask Jesus into their lives. This is seen as the finishing line for people; anything extra is almost a bonus. Yet what were Jesus' instructions to His followers in Matthew? "Go therefore and make disciples of all the nations...teaching them to observe all things that I have commanded you" (Matt. 28:19-20).

When we embrace the Jewishness of Jesus, we can accept the Jewishness of His mission and methods, and understand what He wants for us, too, as individual believers. The emphasis is never just on *arriving* but on *learning* to be a disciple and, as leaders, on *teaching*, not simply *saving*. If salvation is the door, discipleship must be the ongoing journey on the other side of that door.

His Methods

How about the techniques Jesus used to teach and train His disciples? Surely the Savior of man had His own unique methods of teaching the Torah?

In fact, *Jesus used a variety of traditional rabbinical teaching techniques.*

For instance, he used *parables* to illustrate a point. These have a story, or *mashal*, and an interpretation, or *nimshal*.

An example of this was when the prophet Nathan used a parable to trick King David into acknowledging his adultery and murder. He told a story of a lamb, and only when David became incensed at one character's treatment of the lamb did he pull out the hidden meaning and accuse David of similar behavior (see 2 Sam. 12:1-14).

The parables of Jesus often have remarkable parallels in those of other rabbis, both at the time and before. King parables ("There was once a certain king...") were particularly common, for instance.

There is a common rabbinical teaching method called *Kal-va-homer* in Hebrew. This means literally "light and heavy," and might involve expressions such as, "If...then how much more...?" The sense is that if a principle applies in a situation where it is less sure, it must certainly apply in one where it is definite.

An example of this is when Jesus says, "If you then, being evil, know how to give good gifts to your children, how much more will your Father who is in heaven give good things to those who ask Him?" (Matt. 7:11). He is using this technique of developing concepts logically.

Another technique is called *remez* in Hebrew, which means "hint." A rabbi would make reference to a scripture but find the hint of a deeper meaning in it than just the plain interpretation. Often this was in the context and passage from which that Scripture was drawn. Their listeners understood very well what was being said because, knowing the Scriptures far better than we do today, they recognized and understood the significance of the verses alluded to.

Jesus repeatedly referenced specific passages from Scripture. For example, when He said, "Most assuredly, I say to you, before Abraham was, I am" (John 8:58) the listeners became very angry! They recognized that Jesus was alluding to the words God told Moses to say to the children of Israel, to identify that he was truly sent by their God: "'I am who I am.' ...Thus you shall say to the children of Israel, 'I am has sent me to you'" (Exod. 3:14). Jesus was therefore clearly signaling that He was God in human form, and the one who had sent Moses.

Another example is when Jesus said to the weeping women following Him, "If they do these things in the green wood [or tree], what will be done in the dry?" (Luke 23:31). This seems almost mysterious until you realize, even at this awful moment, Jesus continued to use Scripture in this same way. Jesus is referring to Ezekiel 20:47, which talks of a fire consuming green and dry trees, or "wood." Green wood symbolized innocence, and the *Green Tree* had therefore come to be seen as a symbol for the Messiah.

The passage in Ezekiel talks about terrible devastation caused by a forest fire. So Jesus is saying if they are doing this to Me, who is innocent, imagine what they will do to those who are not. He is warning them of the destruction that was to come at the hands of the Romans (Jerusalem was sacked with huge loss of life in AD 70 and the Temple destroyed) and simultaneously signaling that He is the Messiah.

Ignorance of these techniques can lead to all sorts of misunderstandings and misinterpretations. One problem is that our familiarity with the Scriptures that Jesus and the other rabbis alluded to is minimal, certainly compared to the average Jew of the time. For them, the Torah and its interpretation was the basis of all life and culture, so they instantly understood the references.

One area we can misunderstand unless we restore the Jewish context is Jesus' use of questions. We often see Him in the midst of debates and discussions with the religious leaders of the day, the common people, and also with His disciples. We read numerous accounts in the Gospels of debates Jesus had about the correct interpretations of Scripture.

We tend to think that Jesus' disciples asked questions because they were foolish and that asking questions back was His way of dealing with this, or being mysterious. Instead, we must understand it was part of the very fabric of the culture, and the expectation of all rabbis was to have these debates with their students and others.

Often in churches, however, we emphasize the need to *believe* without questioning. We mustn't ask our leaders questions or, even worse, ask God! Yet there is a saying that Jewish fathers traditionally might, after a school day, ask their children not, "Did you learn anything?" but *"Did you ask a good question?"* Do we discourage debate simply because we are worried we won't have the answers?

We read the Bible *alone* and so we think that learning is either about sitting in church listening or is an individual thing, as it generally is in our culture. Yet the context in which Jesus learned and taught was communal *discussion* about the Word of God; this was at the heart of His culture. It was part of His approach to discipleship, and so it must be for us too.

What were Jesus' instructions to His church? Simply to get people to believe in Him? No! "Go therefore and make disciples of all the nations...teaching them to observe all things that I have commanded you" (Matt. 28:19-20). Obedience is about putting teaching into action. Teaching requires debate and inquiry if it is to lead to effective action.

When we restore the Jewishness of His teaching, we can approach the way we learn and teach as modern-day disciples in the same way that Jesus did back then. It becomes clear that just sitting listening to sermons once or twice a week was not the intended or biblical model.

Instead, we must allow discussion, questions, and an interactive approach to discipleship where the *lives* of both discipler and disciple are entwined, not disconnected. Relationship and time were indispensable for the Jewish model of discipleship Jesus used. Without this relationship and interaction, people can become extremely frustrated, struggling to believe what they can't yet understand nor have ever seen demonstrated.

The disciple, traditionally, was aiming to become like his master. As Jesus said, "It's enough for a disciple that he be like his teacher" (Matt. 10:25). For this to happen, the disciple must not only *hear* what the teacher *believes* but *see how they live their life.*

Then the teacher can say, as Paul said, "Imitate me, just as I also imitate Christ" (1 Cor. 11:1). This is very different from standing on a platform and saying, "Believe this!"

There is an interesting parallel with the Israeli army. The officers lead from the front, shouting not 'forward' but *aharai* meaning literally 'after me' or 'follow me'. Because of this they have an unusually high casualty rate among the officers as opposed to the soldiers.

This same principle applies to Christian living. When we return to true discipleship, we will return to a stronger Christianity and build a stronger community of believers. As we know, it's not enough to present Jesus to people, we must *represent* Him as much as we can.

THE TEACHING OF JESUS

The pinnacle, the essence, of "Christian" values, if you like, is captured in the Sermon on the Mount.

The average believer might think Jesus was essentially saying to His audience, "Here is a whole new framework outside of the one you're familiar with. That was then; this is now!"

Except that one of the first things Jesus says in this passage is that He doesn't want His hearers to misunderstand by thinking He has come to *abolish* the Law of Moses or the writings of the prophets (the Torah). Instead, He says He has come to *fulfill* them. He warns His disciples that if they teach anyone to ignore even the smallest commandment from them, they will be called the least in the kingdom of heaven, whereas if they obey and teach others God's commandments, they will be called great.

Which laws is He referring to? Those revealed to the children of Israel through Moses and the prophets, i.e., the Torah.

He then goes even further and says that disciples of His must have a righteousness that exceeds that of the religious leaders, the Pharisees!

What do we do with these statements? I think most of us find them a bit confusing, and so we tend to leave them on the shelf marked "too difficult" (along with passages about the end times and a range of other stuff!).

If we understand the context in which Jesus was speaking, however, things become much clearer and everything starts to make sense.

For it seems that Jesus was entering a common sphere of debate and instruction that rabbis employed. The late biblical scholar Dwight Pryor has outlined this in a way that makes sense of the passage, starting with this seemingly difficult section, and brings it to life.

He explains that the terms *fulfill* and *destroy* are not common to us but were common in rabbinical discourse of the time (and to this day). To "fulfill" God's Word meant to interpret it in such a manner as to make the meaning clear; to "destroy" it meant to interpret it incorrectly.[2]

The Jewish people believed that when the Messiah came He would reveal the truest meaning of the Torah, and Jesus is speaking directly to this idea and confirming it. In this sense, He is doing the very *opposite* of what many of us believe and have been taught—He is establishing the central importance of the Torah!

So Jesus is saying, "Don't misunderstand—I've come to give you the *correct interpretation of God's Word*, so you might *understand* and *apply* it correctly, living it out as the Father *truly* intended, rather than as demonstrated by most of the religious leaders today."

He then goes on, not to give a new set of values but *a renewed and pure interpretation of God's instructions.* The key is that rather than focusing on what is or isn't allowed, He calls us to focus on the *spirit* and purpose of—the intention *behind*—the commandments. The *heart* of them, if you like.

Thus, the whole idea behind the Sermon on the Mount is that we are not to focus on *not breaking* God's commandments but to *go beyond the minimum in keeping them* and see how much we can live out the full *intention* of God's teaching—the heart of it. If we do this, our righteousness will exceed that of the Pharisees—those who Jesus said looked more at the dos and don'ts than the *spirit* of God's Word.

It is as if they lived making sure they didn't overstep the lines at the side of the road. Jesus tells us that this isn't good enough for God, nor was it His intention in giving the Torah. Instead, we are to aim for the center of the road and not worry so much about how close we can get to the barriers before we're off the edge. No one can drive properly like that!

You might say, surely we are not simply trying to keep God's laws in our own strength? Very true. This righteousness Jesus talks about cannot be achieved without the Holy Spirit at work in us, bringing the *spirit* of the Torah commandments alive in us. This is the new covenant Jeremiah prophesied about when he said, "I will put My law in their minds, and write it on their hearts" (Jer. 31:33).

This is the Word becoming flesh in our lives. The Holy Spirit cannot become active in our spirits until we embrace what Jesus did for us on the cross. Until we do, we remain separated from God, whether Jew or Gentile.

We are not, then, trying to establish our own *righteousness*, but rather to *live out* that righteousness that has been won for us and birthed in us. As Paul said, "It is no longer I who live, but Christ lives in me" (Gal. 2:20), and, "it was not I but God who was working through me by his grace" (1 Cor. 15:10 NLT). So the life he is talking about *is* God's life and nature working in and through us.

Paul says the law is like a set of instructions saying, "Do this, don't do this, et cetera" that we will inevitably fail at keeping. Jesus offers a better righteousness, one only found through His sacrifice on the cross. That righteousness is not the abandonment of God's laws, however; rather, it is the very expression of the heart of them through His nature at work in us by His Spirit.

Often I think the problem is that we confuse mercy and grace. Mercy is not receiving a punishment we deserved, and we have received this mercy through Jesus' death. But we also receive grace, which is receiving power and gifts that we *don't* deserve, and this empowerment is to *do something*—to live out the *essence* of the Torah, God's Word, as Jesus described.

In the ongoing process of sanctification, we must allow His teaching to come alive in us so we come closer and closer to living out His Word and His life truly being expressed in and through us. We can then reclaim, if you like, the baby of good works without the bathwater of legalism. The problem is not good works (i.e., a new way of living), which must flow from a renewed, repentant heart. The problem comes when we try to establish our *righteousness* through those works rather than allowing them to flow *from* the righteousness and new life that we have received in Christ.

I hope you can see that as we restore the Jewish lens a new picture begins to emerge of how we need to understand His, and therefore our, mission. We see the details that have been blurred until now—even the lines of detail we never knew were there. We get a clearer understanding of how we are to interpret His teaching and how we are to teach and train others—and a much clearer idea of the continuity that exists between what we call the Old and New Testaments.

There is so much more we could look at concerning the Jewishness of Jesus—of His life, His ministry and teaching, and certainly His death as the Messiah. However, there are other books that do this, and it's beyond the scope of this one to go much further in this area.

In the remaining two chapters of Part One, I want to look at something that goes hand in hand with our picture of Jesus, and that is our picture of His first followers and the early church.

If our picture of Jesus as a Jewish man has been blurred, so has our picture of His followers. Now that we've seen a clearer picture of the Jewish Jesus, we must remind ourselves that the aim of the disciple was to become like his master. When Jesus said, "Follow Me," He was saying, "*Lech Aharai*" or "Walk as I walk," so we would expect to see those first disciples of Jesus doing exactly that.

NOTES

1. *Shabbat*, 31A.
2. Dwight Pryor, *Behold the Man* (Dayton, Ohio: Centre for Judaic Christian Studies, 2005), 91-92. This is from the companion study textbook to the DVD teaching series, Session 9. www.jcstudies.com.

THE JEWISH DISCIPLES

THE APOSTLES AND FIRST BELIEVERS WERE JEWISH

Vatican City lies within the city of Rome, Italy. It is the smallest sovereign state in the world at just 44 hectares and with a population of under 900. It is ruled by the Bishop of Rome, otherwise known as the Pope.

It contains one of the greatest and largest churches in the world, St. Peter's Basilica. People from all over the world come to visit and marvel at its magnificence. Yet how often do the people visiting consider that it is named after a Jewish man who would never have called himself a Christian? Rather, Peter lived and died as a Jewish man, even as a follower of Jesus.

Another Jewish man lent his name to the famous St. Paul's cathedral in London.

When we stop to consider this, is it not striking how little our mental pictures include about the Jewish context of that early church and its leaders?

Jesus talked about His mission as being to the "house of Israel," and it is from these Jewish people that He drew His disciples and chose certain ones to be the apostles, or key leaders.

All of the apostles and the early disciples, then, were Jewish. These formed the original assembly of "called-out ones" or *ekklesia*—the word later translated as "church."

And so the New Testament, like the Old, is composed of historical accounts and letters written by Jewish men, with the probable exception of Luke and Acts (although some scholars believe even he was a Jewish convert). Some were written *to* Jewish people (e.g. Matthew's Gospel and Hebrews), some to non-Jews, and some to both, but all except a very few were written *by* Jews.

In Acts 2, the 3,000 "souls" added to the kingdom on the day of Pentecost were all Jewish. The believers who "were together, and had all things in common" (Acts 2:44) and who continued to meet "daily with one accord in the temple" (Acts 2:46) were all Jewish (no non-Jew was even allowed in the temple). And where it says that "the Lord added to the church daily those who were being saved" (Acts 2:47), this still means Jewish people!

The apostles, we are told, didn't cease to teach and preach daily in the temple and in people's houses (see Acts 5:42)—Jewish apostles, explaining to other Jewish men and women how Jesus was and is the Savior promised to the Jewish people, how to know Him, and how to live together as instructed by Him.

Gentiles Join the Church

In fact, the Gentiles (this just means all people who aren't Jewish) didn't get much of a look-in till chapter 10 of the book of Acts. God gave a Roman centurion called Cornelius a vision and told him to send some men to find Peter in Joppa.

At the same time, God gave Peter a vision of a sheet containing a whole range of animals, some of which were unclean for Jewish people to eat, and then commanded him to eat. Peter, misunderstanding, thought God was telling him to break the commandments of the Torah.

Notice that he states, even several years into the life of the early church, that *he has continued to follow the Jewish dietary laws.* If Peter had *not* been following the Jewish dietary laws, he would have had no confusion.

When Cornelius' servants arrived, it became clear, however, that God was referring not to actual food but to *people,* encouraging Peter to go with Cornelius' men. Finally, Peter went with them, and Cornelius and his whole household received both the Gospel and the baptism of the Holy Spirit, with the gift of speaking in tongues.

Peter and the other Jewish believers were amazed. *"And those of the circumcision* [the Jews] *who believed were astonished...because the gift of the Holy Spirit had been poured out on the Gentiles also"* (Acts 10:45).

For them, even with the prophecies of Scripture and Jesus Himself, this was a momentous and confusing turn of events. Those who believed in Jesus were receiving promises made by God to the *Jewish* people over centuries. How could someone who wasn't Jewish get in on the act?

It is interesting to note that even in this episode, Luke stresses how Cornelius loved and blessed the Jewish people. This is actually given as part of the justification for his receiving the Gospel and gift of the Holy Spirit!

When Peter goes to Jerusalem and meets up with the other "apostles and brethren," he must defend what has happened. They are outraged at first that he went to eat with these non-Jews, which was forbidden. Peter has to remind them of the words of Jesus that His disciples would be baptized with the Holy Spirit. If these non-Jews have experienced the same baptism, they must also be able to be followers of the Jewish Messiah. How strange!

A key verse is Acts 11:17: "If therefore God gave them *the same gift as He gave us* when we believed on the Lord Jesus Christ, who was I that I could withstand God?"

It says that at this they became silent and then, seemingly awestruck, said, "Then God has *also* granted to the Gentiles repentance to life" (Acts 11:18).

Later, in Acts 15:16-17, James quotes Amos 9:11-12 as another scriptural explanation and justification of what is happening.

> *Afterward I will return and restore the fallen house of David. I will rebuild its ruins and restore it, so that* ***the rest of humanity*** *might seek the Lord,* ***including the Gentiles****—all those I have called to be mine* (NLT).

We see three key points here:

- First, the whole early believing community (church) was Jewish, both in Jerusalem and beyond.

- Second, they continued to live as Jews, which meant they followed God's commandments and teachings in the Torah (*after* they had received the Holy Spirit).
- Third, there is an "also," referring to the Gentiles who became part of the church community.

We see the words "also" and "until" time and again in both the New and Old Testaments. Too often, though, the church has replaced "also" with "instead," and ignored the word "until" altogether. We will examine both in more detail later because they are key to our understanding.

The Early Church

When we think of that early church, the first thing we think of is not a group of Jewish people, living as Jews, in the knowledge that they had found their Messiah.

I think somehow we have a picture in our minds of a modern-day church, following "Christian" holidays, maybe even Christmas and Easter and all the other traditions we associate with Christianity. Perhaps they were even thinking about where they could build their first church building, with a great spire!

Instead, the true picture is of a group of Jewish people following Jewish traditions and attempting to live out the essence of God's commandments in the Torah. They were empowered by the Holy Spirit, living in the freedom of salvation and the new life offered through their Messiah, the greatest rabbi, who had made the ultimate sacrifice so that they could experience the love of God directly for themselves. They were utterly bemused when God first began to touch these Gentiles.

As more Gentiles came into the community, this new situation created a dilemma: should the non-Jews have to follow the whole of the Torah or not? *Should they have to live as Jews?*

In Acts 15:1-29, we read what happened. Verse 6 says that the "apostles and elders came together to consider this matter." The conclusion they came to, with some vigorous argument from Peter, is in verses 23-29. They wrote a letter to "the brethren who are of the Gentiles in Antioch, Syria and Cilicia," telling them that they didn't need to observe the whole Torah, only to abstain from "things offered to idols, from blood, from things strangled, and from sexual immorality."

Their reasoning was that, as Jews, they had heard the Torah preached and taught week in, week out, for generations. The Gentiles joining the church had, however, no such experience. Therefore, they were *releasing the non-Jews from any need to follow the detailed instructions of the Torah or to live precisely as the Jews lived.*

The implications of this passage are vital. They clearly did not consider following the Torah ("Law") *a bad thing.* Quite the opposite. This fits with everything Jesus said during His ministry and that we looked at earlier about Him not coming to "abolish" the Law but to "fulfill" or interpret it correctly.

It also makes more sense when we understand the correct meaning of *Torah.* It is more about instruction and teaching than just abstract "laws." Remember that these believers were led by the key leaders whom Jesus taught and to whom He passed His ministry.

The Jews clearly *did* follow the Torah, as other Jews of the time, or else why make this special exception for the Gentiles? Why not just say, "This is how we Christians live, so live like us"?

This point is made very clear later on, in Acts 21:15-36. Paul goes up to Jerusalem and tells James and all the elders about what God has been doing through him among the Gentiles. They are very excited, and in turn tell Paul "how many myriads of Jews there are who have believed, and they are all *zealous for the law* [Torah]" (Acts 21:20). Clearly, they all continued to study and follow the Torah.

They then tell Paul that some people have been saying that "you teach all the Jews who are among the Gentiles to forsake Moses, saying they ought not to circumcise their children nor walk according to the customs" (Acts 21:21).

They suggest that, in order to show that these rumors are false, Paul take four men who have taken a vow, and pay their expenses so that they may shave their heads, "and that all may know that those things of which they were informed concerning you are nothing, *but that you yourself also walk orderly and keep the law* [Torah]" (Acts 21:24). Paul promptly follows their instructions. Indeed, Paul himself takes a similar vow later on in Acts.

From the above we can see that either Paul himself followed the law (Torah commandments followed by the Jews) or he was a complete hypocrite and deceiver. Yet most of us would never think of the great founder of Christian theology as following the Torah!

Indeed, *the very act of trying to prove his Torah-observant credentials to other Jews is what led to Paul's final arrest, imprisonment, and, ultimately, death.*

We see in verse 29 that it was a false accusation, based on a misunderstanding by some Jews from Asia. They mistakenly assumed Paul had brought a non-Jew into the temple, in contradiction of the Torah commandments. *The passage makes clear that this was untrue.*

This picture of Paul and the early followers of Jesus seems so different from the one we have in our minds when we imagine them, yet all this makes perfect sense, given what we have looked at earlier. If Peter and the others, and then many more including Paul, had become disciples of Jesus, we would expect them to want to become like Him. And if He had taught on how to live out God's Torah perfectly, then we would expect them to be doing the same.

So how did the church change and lose this sense of its own Jewish roots and identity, and how can we get them back?

CHAPTER 6

Restoring the Jewish Lens

How the Church Lost Its Jewish Roots

Key questions for the early Jewish church leaders, as we have seen, were, "How can anyone who is not Jewish be part of this community?" and, "If they are a member, how much should they have to live as us Jews?" They also had to ask themselves, "How should we Jews live together with these Gentiles in a way that is pleasing to God?"

Much of the New Testament reflects how they wrestled with these issues, which are so alien to us today.

Over the following centuries, however, as the Gospel spread and the majority of people in the church were now *Gentiles,* the question turned around. The non-Jewish church members wrestled with the opposite questions: *how could someone who was Jewish and joining the church continue to live as a Jew and be part of "their" community? How much should they have to abandon their Jewish customs and Torah observance and live instead as Gentiles?*

Tragically, the church began to answer these new questions without the same grace or understanding as the apostles and early leaders had. They decided that Jews should have to abandon their Jewishness, despite finding their Jewish King and Messiah, and despite the adherence of all those first members of the church to the Torah.

The more it lost touch with its Jewish roots, the more the church began to develop a mindset completely at variance with that of the early church community. Jews were expected to abandon their Jewish beliefs, customs, and observance. For surely, it was reasoned, we are now "free from the Law." The subtleties of Paul's arguments—of what it was that followers of Jesus were actually free from, for instance, and of how this new community should look—were obscured or altogether lost.

Paul talks in his letter to the Ephesians about how God has made "one new man" from two peoples, the Jews and the Gentiles. Yet he also talks elsewhere about the distinctions between Jews and Gentiles. The church began to lose sight of this idea of distinctiveness within a unified community (which we will explore in Part Three). It was replaced with the idea of uniformity—where everyone had to conform to one way of being and one set of traditions.

Over the centuries, spurred on by the anti-Judaic, even anti-Semitic teachings of key church leaders such as Ignatius, Origen, and John Chrysostom, the church became more and more hostile toward the idea of its Jewish roots. Rather than seeing them as the platform for their faith, they saw them as unimportant and, worse, as a burden. The church became totally opposed to the idea of Jewish believers living as Jews. This developed into outright hostility toward the Jews and toward even the idea of *anything* Jewish infiltrating the church.

Jews who chose to follow their Messiah and accepted the promised gift of new life and the Holy Spirit were now expected by the church to renounce all things Jewish. They were therefore expected to turn their back on celebrating any of the Jewish (biblical) holidays or festivals that God had commanded them to celebrate—the ones that those first believers and the early church celebrated. Instead, they were expected to follow the newly created "Christian" customs, rituals, traditions, and holidays.

The Jewish, biblical calendar was ultimately abandoned in favor of the Roman calendar, festivals were often aligned to existing pagan ones, and practices relating to pagan religions were incorporated into the church. New traditions were created and elevated as central, while the biblical traditions and festivals were considered defunct, worthless, and even morally debased.

Some of this actually related to the needs of rulers and politicians to more easily rule their citizens using a framework their people could relate to. A turning point, for instance, came when the Roman emperor Constantine adopted Christianity. A little later, in AD 380, Emperor Theodosius made Christianity the state religion of Rome. The church, and therefore the Empire, became even more hostile toward all things Jewish around this time.

Ultimately, this severing paved the way for the direct persecution of the Jews—for instance, the torture, death, and forced "conversion" of Jews in the Inquisition, as well as the kind of anti-Semitism that led to the Holocaust. In fact, many waves of persecution followed over the centuries. Jews were often portrayed by the church as allied to Satan—a depraved, twisted, and hopelessly unredeemable people!

My great-grandparents, for example, came to England to escape the *pogroms*—widespread persecution of Jews that took place across much of the western Russian Empire (incorporating areas such as Poland, Belarus, Lithuania, and Ukraine) at the turn of the century. For an account of anti-Semitism in the church over the centuries, Michael Brown's book *Our Hands Are Stained with Blood* is exceptional, if distressing.

It is a sad and terrible fact that for many centuries the worst persecutor of the Jewish people was the very faith community that they had birthed, founded on the Jewish Bible, following the Jewish Messiah, the King of the Jews, and clinging to the teachings of His Jewish apostles. All this despite Paul's assertion that the Jews, even non-believers in Jesus, are nonetheless "beloved for the sake of the fathers" (Rom. 11:28). How far and how often the church has strayed from the truth of God's heart in this area.

SEEING THROUGH THE JEWISH LENS

Once we strip back the layers of our tradition and restore a more accurate picture of the apostles and early believing community, we can see the role of the Jewish people in a new light.

The inclusion of non-Jews in the church actually led to all sorts of new questions and dilemmas about how Jews and Gentiles should live together. It was the Jewish leaders, the apostles, who wrestled with these on our behalf. Many of the New Testament letters contain discussions about these very issues, much of which we then apply to ourselves. *Yet so often we forget the original context.*

When we do, we can lose sight of what is really being discussed. We simply apply the bits we like and ignore the rest, especially the difficult or challenging bits! *In reality, we are eavesdropping on a conversation we only partially understand.*

We should remember that the Gospel accounts themselves are full of issues and references that only make sense once we restore the Jewishness of what we are reading. Let me illustrate.

Remember the story of the man born blind from birth in John 9? John describes in great detail exactly what happened to him. First Jesus heals him; then the man finds himself hauled before the religious leaders, who desperately try to convince him that he wasn't really blind from birth!

Note that they aren't saying he is lying about the healing itself. It's just the fact that he was *born* blind rather than *becoming* blind that they are disputing. They even question his parents. The reason for this is only apparent if we know the Jewish context.

Miracles were not unique to Jesus. The Bible itself contains accounts of all sorts of miracles (for example, those performed by Elijah and Elisha), including healings and even resurrections.

However, the scholar Arnold Fruchtenbaum explains why this particular miracle became so contentious and why John therefore writes so much about it in his Gospel.

Fruchtenbaum explains that according to rabbinic tradition certain miracles could only be performed by the true Messiah and would be a sign of His coming. One of these was for Him to heal someone who had been born blind.[1]

Hence this becomes the point of contention, for if the man was born blind Jesus has shown everyone that He is the Messiah! The religious leaders knew this, and so did everyone else. This explains the desperate attempts of the religious leaders to get the man to change his story and makes sense of why John presents us with so much more detail than most other miracles. He devotes an entire chapter of His Gospel to it. As he says later on:

> *The disciples saw Jesus do many other miraculous signs in addition to the ones recorded in this book. But these are written so that you may continue to believe that Jesus is the Messiah, the Son of God* (John 20:30-31 NLT).

Jesus and Passover

Let me present another example. For the early church, the death and resurrection of Jesus were the fulfillment of the Passover festival rather than a separate festival called Easter. In fact, in most languages the name for Easter is actually some variant of the Greek word for Passover, *Pascha*.

God commanded the Jewish people to celebrate the Passover each year to commemorate their escape from slavery in Egypt. We read about it in Exodus 12. In verse 24 God says specifically:

> *Remember, these instructions are a permanent law that you and your descendants must observe forever* (NLT).

Every Passover the Jewish people remember how the blood of a lamb, sprinkled on the doorpost of each family's house, meant that God spared their ancestors from the angel of death that killed all the firstborn sons in Egypt. This was the final plague that led to the Israelites' release by Pharaoh. Each Jewish person is instructed to celebrate and commemorate the Passover as though they, personally, had been the ones spared and delivered from Egypt.

This deliverance from Egypt is the foundational event in the formation of the people of Israel. When Jewish people celebrate the Passover they remember that they were once slaves with no hope, but that God rescued them, made them His people, and brought them into His promises and Promised Land.

For the early Jewish believers, the notion of Jesus as the Lamb of God related completely to this story of the Passover, which they felt had found its prophetic fulfillment in Jesus' death on the cross and the power of His blood applied to their lives.

This is why Paul likens baptism to the Israelites entering and then coming up out of the Red Sea, their enemies utterly destroyed behind them and their new life ahead of them. Just like the crossing of the Red Sea, baptism happens *after* the escape from Egypt, or salvation.

When we look closely at the Passover account, the symbolism is incredible. For the early Jewish believers, this brought the whole story of the crucifixion and resurrection its power, its meaning, and its context. This is what John the Baptist was referring to when he said of Jesus, "Behold! the Lamb of God who takes away the sin of the world!" (John 1:29).

As followers of Jesus, we are mostly oblivious to all this, which is a shame as it brings tremendous richness to our understanding of what He has done for us. It tells us that, truly, it is only through His blood that we are saved, just as the Israelites were. It highlights the importance of His perfection, because the lambs for the Passover had to be perfect. Just as the lambs were examined by the priests for defects, so Jesus was examined by the high priest for fault, and none was found.

Now, I grew up celebrating Passover every year with my family and extended family. Some of my earliest memories are of Seder nights (the Passover meal and service) with all of the traditional foods, the unleavened bread (*matzoh*), and the different dishes on the table, each with its significance.

The service goes through the story of the exodus from Egypt. We would drink the different cups of wine (yes, folks, we've lost a lot!) with the lamb shank in the center of the table representing the lambs that were slain to save the Israelite families.

All of my childhood I did this and still do today. Yet only after years of being in church and through my own study did I begin to understand the associations with Easter, the representation of Jesus as that Lamb, and the power behind the whole story.

I believe that there is a great cost to *every* believer, Jewish or not, if they don't understand the foundations and true meaning of their faith. This loss is a natural consequence of the abandonment of the Jewish roots that I described previously, for if we decide the "old" is all things Jewish and is done away with entirely, then the "Old Testament" is barely worth reading at all. The Passover theme so clearly outlined in the Torah is lost to us. So is a sense of fulfillment and continuity. In its place comes an event and a tradition out of context.

Worse still, the church increasingly tried to *discourage and forbid anyone*, even those who were Jewish, from following the same pattern as the early Jewish believers. For Jewish people today, this means that what could be presented in the context of what they know and understand is instead presented as something completely new and alien.

Jews know that God has commanded them to celebrate and remember the Passover "forever." They know their Messiah wouldn't cancel the Word of God to them but would fully reveal its meaning and purpose. If they knew that that Lamb was not a *different* sacrifice but the very fulfillment of the Passover story, then perhaps they would more easily relate to their Messiah. They might understand that we are continuing to celebrate the fact that, through the blood of this Lamb, death has truly "passed us over."

Jesus and the Torah

It is true that there are some passages in Paul's writing that seem to indicate that the Law is "done away with." It's beyond the scope of this book to examine all of these in detail, although we will look at some later.

However, what is clear is that if Jesus said anyone teaching a disciple to break the least, tiniest element of the Law would be called "least in the kingdom of heaven" (Matt. 5:19), then we either need to revise our ideas of Paul as a great man or look again at this aspect of his teaching. If Paul went to great pains to demonstrate that he didn't break or teach against the Torah, as the Jews were claiming he did, then it would seem sensible to read and understand anything else in the light of this very clear fact presented to us by the writer of Acts.

The strange thing is that the church has essentially credited Paul with doing the very thing that he was accused of all those centuries ago—abandoning the Torah and teaching other Jews to do the same. It was for defending himself against this charge that, ultimately, he was killed.

The death of Jesus on our behalf gives us access to an amazing forgiveness, to mercy, and to grace—all by definition undeserved. This grace empowers us to live out the commands of God, summed up by love, and to build a community that reflects Him fully and shines His light to the world.

Gentiles are not called to live as Jews, nor to slavishly try to follow the details of the Torah commandments, but let's not throw out the baby of *learning* with the bathwater of *legalism*. We must REWIRE our thinking so we don't allow the labels "Old Testament" and "New Testament" to misdirect our understanding of God's teaching. We need to learn the keys and principles that the Torah holds and understand how to live these out in the light of the teachings of Jesus and His followers. When we do this, so much of the Bible will become more alive, more understandable, and more powerful.

Correct context leads to correct interpretation, and correct interpretation leads to correct application. This will not stifle but only *enhance* the abundant, fulfilled life that Jesus promised to His followers in John 10:10.

The implications of all this for Jewish people are huge also. It means that to follow Jesus—or *Yeshua*, to give Him His Jewish name—is not to either abandon Jewishness or to completely ignore the Torah.

I cannot, even as a Jew, say exactly what this looks like, for that model was lost through the process I outlined earlier. Like most believers who are Jews, though, I am always in the process of discovering what it could look like, recovering my buried Jewish inheritance, and trying to make it a blessing for others rather than a stick to beat them with.

I can say this from my experience: the Gospel redefines our relationship to the Torah—to the Bible itself. We have a Messiah and Savior who has accomplished for us what we could never accomplish through legalistic observance.

The author N.T. Wright sums it up this way in his book *Justification*:

> Paul's entire understanding of the Mosaic law is that it never was intended as a ladder of good works up which one might climb to earn the status of "righteousness." It was given, yes, as the way of life (Romans 7:10), but it was the way of life for *a people already redeemed*...God did not say to Israel in Egypt, "Here is my Torah; if you keep

> it perfectly for a year or two, then I will liberate you from your slavery," but "I am liberating you now because I promised Abraham I would do so; when, and only when, I have done so, I will give you the way of life that you will need for when you come into your promised land." ...The Torah, the Mosaic law, was never given or intended as a means whereby either an individual or the nation as a whole might, through obedience, earn liberation from slavery, redemption, rescue, salvation, "righteousness" or whatever else. The gift always preceded the obligation. This is how Israel's covenant theology worked.[2]

Jesus gave us an important principle—a lens through which we can look at this. In relation to the Sabbath, He said, "The Sabbath was made for man, and not man for the Sabbath" (Mark 2:27). So those arguing about the detail of what did and didn't constitute Sabbath observance were missing the point, turning a blessing provided by God into a burden.

However, the principles in the Sabbath are incredibly powerful—the need to take rest, to trust God in that, and to provide rest for employees and animals. All these things help us to create a more just society, to develop stronger, more balanced families with deeper relationships, and so on.

So while God will not punish us for not resting, it's easy to see how working seven days a week, or forcing others to, could limit the blessings and fruitfulness in our lives as well as theirs. It is also a potential source of tremendous injustice and oppression.

We can find forgiveness and intimacy with our Father God and be free to explore what the Torah can teach us about how to live lives that are pleasing to God as we follow the teachings of the greatest rabbi of them all. To paraphrase Him, we might say, "Man was not given for the Torah, but the Torah was given for man."

It's true that some parts are harder to understand, seem archaic, and are difficult to apply practically. Some seem to be clearly related to the specific needs of the culture they were originally given to. But we need to start with the right principles and seek wisdom in applying the keys to our lives rather than avoid it on that basis.

It provided the foundation and framework for all of Jesus' life and teaching. He was not simply a philosopher. Likewise, it provided the framework for the teaching of Jesus' followers, who built the church and wrote the stories and letters that make up the New Testament.

Conclusion

If we want to understand the character and teaching of Jesus and His followers, we need to read the New Testament differently. We need to let go of tradition and restore the Jewish context in which they lived and thought.

This will cause us to reconnect with the whole Bible, and especially with the Old Testament, in fresh ways. When we reattach parts one and two of the Bible, the "Old Testament" and "New Testament," Scriptures that seemed archaic will become a new source of insight and revelation.

We will more easily understand their relevance for our lives today and their connection with the thoughts and words of Jesus and His followers.

When we put on this Jewish lens, passages that seemed obscure in the New Testament will come alive. Verses that seemed contradictory will make sense. A whole new level of detail will appear. Above all, we will come to know Jesus more authentically and intimately than ever before.

We cannot be sentimental about revising our views of Scripture and the assumptions we have made, for our desire is surely to live out the truest expression of our faith, and faith comes alive when we hear God through all of His Word as He intended to be heard, not the way our culture or traditions tell us.

When you see Jesus in this way, it will transform your walk with Him. It will give you a deeper revelation of who He is. So I want to challenge you and ask you a question: why settle for the headlines and blurred vision when you can have so much more?

If we want to develop a complete picture, however, I believe we must not stop here but go further and look at another, perhaps even more contentious area, and that is the whole subject of Israel, the Jewish people, and the relationship of both to the church.

I believe that to restore our understanding of the Jewish Jesus without restoring our understanding of His heart for His Jewish brothers and sisters, whom we know as Israel, is to only have a fraction of the picture.

We have seen that Jesus continues to define Himself by His Jewish identity throughout the Bible. He and the other writers of the New Testament have much to tell us about the subject of Israel, both the people and the land.

This is what we shall explore in Part Two.

NOTES

1. Arnold G. Fruchtenbaum, *The Three Messianic Miracles* (Tustin, CA: Ariel Ministries, 1983), 14-21.
2. N.T. Wright, *Justification: God's Plan & Paul's Vision* (Downers Grove, IL: IVP Academic, 2009), 232.

PART TWO

The Truth about Israel

CHAPTER 7

God Created and Chose Israel

In Chapter 2 we looked at how the journey of Joseph prefigures the life of Jesus. For years, the Egyptians and the surrounding nations saw Joseph simply as their savior, the one who had rescued them from death in the famine.

When the time came and he revealed himself to his natural brothers, everyone saw and heard how deeply he loved his family. It was God's purpose that sent Joseph ahead to Pharaoh's palace, yet Joseph still carried a deep love for his father and brothers, even though they had betrayed him.

In just the same way, once we restore the Jewish lens to our view of Jesus and the early church, it follows that we need to consider God's relationship with the Jewish people and the nation of Israel. Does He still have any plans for this people and nation that we read about throughout our Bible?

I said that part of the blessing of restoring the Jewish context of the New Testament is that we see the humanity of Jesus so much more clearly. With this in mind, we need to explore how He feels about His natural family. Are they just a footnote to Him now?

The Old and New Testaments primarily describe events relating to the Jewish people that took place in Israel. People from all over the world visit the land of Israel to see the places they have read about in their Bibles.

It is amazing to walk on the slopes of the hills around the Sea of Galilee (really a big lake), knowing that you are essentially in the place where Jesus taught the multitudes His interpretation of God's Word.

As you stand next to the giant wall that was originally the supporting wall for the Second Temple (referred to as the Western or "Wailing" Wall by the Jewish people today), it is impossible not to imagine the incredible sight it would have been as centuries of our biblical history played out in this one place—from Solomon's coronation as king in the First Temple all the way through to those first gatherings of the followers of Jesus in the courts of the Second Temple.

Even today we can go and stand on the same Temple Mount and look out across Jerusalem. We can travel across this tiny country and see site after site where the Bible stories we read actually took place. But is this just nostalgia? Is it just a romantic trip to a place that stirs our emotions and brings to life our religious stories? Or is there some enduring significance to this land and the people for whom God called it the promised land?

Paul said in Romans 11:25, "I do not desire, brethren, that you should be ignorant of this mystery, lest you should be wise in your own opinion, that blindness in part has happened to Israel until the fullness of the Gentiles has come in." He says this in the midst of three long chapters (Romans 9, 10, and 11) in which he also goes into painstaking detail about the subject of Israel.

The language he uses is interesting. He says that the Jewish people have experienced a *blindness* in part. Blindness means something is stopping you from seeing. He warns the Gentile believers, however, not to be *ignorant*. Ignorance is just a lack of awareness. Paul saw the dangers of this ignorance entering the church.

He was talking primarily to *non-Jewish (Gentile)* followers of Jesus, saying, "I don't want you to be ignorant of these issues relating to the Jewish people. I want you to understand the church's (and therefore your) relationship to them, and to understand the truth about God's heart and plans in relation to Israel." In general, though, and for most of the last 1,800-plus years, we have been very much ignorant of *exactly* these things! So much so, that far from being informed, we have little or no understanding of even the *relevance* of this subject.

More often it is viewed as an optional side salad or a novelty subject—perhaps something for just a small group of dedicated (and sometimes very vocal!) believers. Paul says, however, that he wants *everyone* to understand it, and if it is really only ignorance stopping us, that means there is no actual barrier and the only requirement for change is a desire to know more.

Paul also says that this subject is a *mystery*. Some of the other things referred to as mysteries are the Gospel, Christ in us, the kingdom of God, and God Himself (see Eph. 6:19; Col. 1:27; Mark 4:11; Col. 2:2). With all these mysteries, it is not a question of God *hiding* the truth. Rather, the very point is that it is His desire to *reveal* it to us. The Gospel is a mystery, but God wants to continue to reveal more and more about it to us. In the same way, God wants our understanding of His purposes for Israel to develop more and more.

Mysteries in the Bible can only be understood by revelation. We cannot simply work them out with our heads, or else they aren't mysteries. This is not like a whodunit, where we can, if we're clever enough, work out who the killer is! It is something that can only be properly understood with the help of the Holy Spirit, and He will help us *if we are willing.*

The mystery referred to in Romans 11:25, however, is so much neglected in the teaching, and therefore understanding, of the church that most of us are not only *ignorant* but also extremely *confused* in relation to the issue of Israel.

Before we go further, let's clarify what we're talking about, because the name "Israel" can refer to different things in different contexts.

In the Bible, "Israel" refers collectively to the Jewish people. This is fundamentally whom Paul is referring to in Romans 11:25. It is also used as a term for the *nation* composed of this people group and, at certain times, for just one specific part of it. Finally, it is used to refer to the land itself where the people lived.

Israel is also the name of the country found today in that region. Modern Israel is a democratic country composed in varying degrees of Jews, Arabs, and a range of other people groups. It seems to be the most talked about and contentious land on the planet, and so we need to understand what (if any) role God might have in this, and what relevance it has for us.

Let's therefore first establish some foundations from Scripture about this whole subject.

God Created Israel

The first thing we need to understand is that *God Himself created Israel for His purposes.*

"Israel" can refer to both the people and the land, although, as we will see, these are inextricably linked in the Bible. Later, we will examine God's promises relating to the land itself, but first we will focus on Israel as a people, and this is the Jewish people we have been talking about. This is actually the primary biblical meaning of "Israel," for *they became a people before they were given a land.*

For the average believer, the story of Israel is something we know is found in the Old Testament. Most people know the famous stories—Moses and the Red Sea, Joseph and his "dream coat" in Egypt, Daniel and the lions' den—because they've become part of our cultural landscape or because they heard them in Sunday school.

However, there seems to be little connection in our minds between these stories and our understanding of our own faith. We see the whole Israel "thing" as vaguely interesting but essentially irrelevant to our understanding of the Gospel. Moreover, we have in our minds the idea that Israel is related to the *law* and works, whereas Christianity is all about *grace* and God's unmerited choosing. This is one of the traditions that we need to reexamine because *Israel was created and chosen by God. It did not choose or create itself.*

Israel was not born out of its own efforts, but out of God's promise to Abraham, which we see in Genesis 12:1-3:

> *Now the Lord had said to Abram: "Get out of your country, from your family and from your father's house, to a land that I will show you. I will make you a great nation; I will bless you and make your name great; and you shall be a blessing. I will bless those who bless you, and I will curse him who curses you; and in you all the families of the earth shall be blessed."*

God repeated these promises to Isaac in Genesis 26:23-24 and to Jacob in Genesis 28:10-15. In Isaiah 43:1, God says, "But now, thus says the Lord, *who created you, O Jacob*, and He who formed you, O Israel." In this context, Jacob is simply another name for Israel.

In Isaiah 44:1-2, He says, "Yet hear now, O Jacob My servant, and Israel whom *I have chosen*. Thus says the Lord *who made you and formed you* from the womb."

In Deuteronomy 26:18-19, it says of Israel, "The Lord has proclaimed you to be His special people...a holy people," and in Isaiah 44:21 God says of Israel, "I have formed thee" (KJV).

So we see clearly that God *created and chose Israel.*

Notice however—*Israel was created and chosen by Him before the Law was given.* It was not chosen just to abstractly follow His commandments, but God specifically says He chose and created Israel *for His own purposes. He gave the Israelites the teaching of the Torah afterward, to help them to fulfill those purposes, not as an end in themselves.*

It is God who initiates. Jesus said, "You did not choose Me, but I chose you" (John 15:16). *In the same way, God chose Israel; Israel did not choose God. Abram's faith was, as ours is, a response to God's choosing.*

The commandments were given *after* this creation, as an instruction manual for the nation—a covenant and constitution laying out God's expectations and promises for the people, as well as warnings about the results of straying from these.

It was not Abram who spontaneously decided to leave Ur and become a new nation called Israel. God said to him, "Get out of your father's house and from your country *and I will make of you a great nation*" (see Gen. 12:1-2).

Psalm 147:20 says, "He has not dealt thus with any nation." In other words, Israel alone among all the nations of the world is somehow unique in the way God deals with it. Time and again we see that God repeats this. *Although the whole world is His, He has chosen this special people for a particular purpose of His and calls them "My people."*

Sometimes Christians have not liked this idea of Israel as a special nation, chosen by God for His purposes. The irony is that this is exactly the complaint the world often has about Christians—that we claim a uniqueness for our faith and claim that we have been chosen by the very Creator of the universe as His special people!

It is almost as if we are afraid that if Israel and the Jewish people are special to God, that means we might be less so. This, of course, simply means that we misunderstand God's heart.

Note that *God says He didn't choose Israel because they were a big or impressive people—quite the opposite.* He says that He chose a small, seemingly insignificant people in order to demonstrate His greatness more effectively.

Echoing this, Paul tells us that "God has chosen the foolish things of the world to shame the wise, and God has chosen the weak things of the world to shame the things which are strong" (1 Cor. 1:27 NASB).

Just as we were not chosen on the basis of our goodness but as an expression of God's love, so the same is true of Israel.

God Called Israel

God is purposeful, and He creates for a purpose. With His choosing comes *responsibility* and *accountability.*

God chose Israel out of all the nations of the earth and decided to use them as a special example for everyone, like a pupil who is called up to stand in front of the class. You remember the mixed feelings you have in that moment—half excited at the idea of being chosen, half anxious in case you make a fool of yourself in front of everyone? Well, this might be one way to think of what God has done with Israel.

In Exodus 19:5-6, God explains clearly and simply His call for the nation of Israel. He says:

> *If you will indeed obey My voice and keep My covenant, then you shall be a special treasure to Me above all people; for all the earth is Mine.* ***And you shall be to Me a kingdom of priests and a holy nation.***

Holy means set apart for His glory and purposes. A priest is a mediator between God and man. The whole of God's dealings with Israel must be understood in this light—that He has created them and chosen them for this task, and He provides for them, talks to them, and blesses and judges them on this basis. He does not bless them randomly, nor is the call abstract. They are to represent Him to the rest of the world.

Just as God said to Abraham that all the nations of the earth would be blessed through him and his descendants, we see that *God demonstrates His nature and character through His relationship with the Jewish people.*

If this call sounds familiar, it is because, as we will see, their call is every believer's call. 1 Peter 2:9 says that believers are "a chosen generation, a royal priesthood, a holy nation, His own special people," clearly echoing Exodus 19. Peter's letter was addressed to Jewish believers, who would have instantly recognized this reference.

Paul said to the Corinthian church, "For consider your calling, brethren, that there were not many wise according to the flesh, not many mighty, not many noble" (1 Cor. 1:26 NASB). A phrase you may have heard is this: "God doesn't call the qualified; He qualifies the called." This is as true of Israel as it is of us as individual followers of Jesus.

Before we go any further, however, let's consider God's heart in all this, because God is not an impassionate planner, soullessly pulling the strings behind the scenes. He is emotionally involved in all that happens, as we would expect if we are made in His image.

So we must ask ourselves a simple question: if God created, chose, and called Israel, how does He *feel* about Israel? For we are to carry His heart in all things.

CHAPTER 8

God Loves Israel

It is impossible to understand what it is like to have a child until you actually experience it. People with children had said this to me so many times and I'd always thought they were exaggerating. Only when Denise and I had Isaac Victor Hoffbrand did I fully get what they were saying.

We recently celebrated Isaac's first birthday, and it was a magical day. We took him for his first haircut, went to the local bakery, and walked in the sunshine on the beachfront. Later, we went with our friends and their similarly aged child to a local zoo.

It was so beautiful watching Isaac and Hugo seeing the animals in the flesh for the first time, and so many they had never even seen a picture of.

"Baaa!" screamed Isaac excitedly as he saw his first real-life, fluffy sheep (which he thankfully avoided trying to sink his teeth into, unlike every toy sheep he had come across).

This love is unlike anything I have experienced before, because never before have I been anyone's "dada." Never before has anyone been so totally dependent on me, or been so unfeasibly cute and adorable in my eyes, or looked at me with such a trusting expression. I'm sure every parent knows what I am talking about.

The thought of anything bad happening to Isaac is so hard to endure. Even though I know challenges and trials will come to him, I am already thinking of ways to help him get through them and come out the other side a bigger, stronger person on the inside. There are no lengths I wouldn't go to in order to protect him.

Occasionally, as he furniture-surfs around the couches in our lounge, he might fall and hurt himself. Even the harm he might cause *himself*, now or by his later choices, causes me to feel grief for him.

Moreover, this love is something that Denise and I share in a way no one else ever truly can. We are now bound together, not just by our own covenant before God and our love for one another, but by our shared love for Isaac and commitment to helping him grow up to be the very best man he can be.

This doesn't mean every moment is easy, nor that there aren't challenges ahead, but whatever lies ahead, I know that it will not diminish our love for him.

In the same way, God doesn't just say that He created, chose, and called Israel; He also makes it very clear that He *loves* Israel, and not just like a friend or acquaintance. Again and again He reaffirms this love. And I believe it is a love that He wants to share with us.

In Zechariah 2:8, He says, "He who touches you [Israel] touches the apple of His eye." The "apple" means the pupil, one of the most precious and sensitive parts of the body. If someone pokes us in the eye, it is an involuntary reflex to close our eyes and fend it off. We simply can't help it.

In Isaiah 43:3-4, He says, "For I am the Lord your God, the Holy One of Israel, your Savior.... Since you were precious in My sight, you have been honored, and I have loved you."

Israel is referred to as "My beloved" and "My firstborn son," among other things.

In Jeremiah 31:3, God says of Israel, "I have loved you, my people, with an everlasting love. With unfailing love I have drawn you to myself" (NLT).

However frustrated God gets with Israel, however disobedient to Him they are, time and again we see in the Bible that God comes back to this key truth—*He loves Israel!* Even when He allows nations to be instruments of His discipline against Israel, He then brings them into judgment. He's like a parent who will discipline their son or daughter, but woe betide anyone else who raises a hand against them!

In case we think God loved them in the past but no longer, Paul says in Romans 11:28, "Many of the people of Israel are now enemies of the Good News, and this benefits you Gentiles. Yet they are still the people he loves because he chose their ancestors Abraham, Isaac, and Jacob" (NLT).

The Bible again and again says that God has *chesed* (pronounced with a guttural, throaty "H" sound at the beginning and usually translated "lovingkindness") toward Israel. One way to think about this is that God has *invested* so much in Israel. He loves them as a people, not just as individuals. Moreover, the two key groups He says He loves in this way are the church and Israel.

In Isaiah 62, God talks about Israel as His bride. Again, we, the church or "called-out ones," are also called out to be His bride.

Let's think of this in another way. We as believers are married to the Lord, and in a marriage you learn to love what the other person loves. There are many things that I appreciate more since knowing Denise. Moreover, if I want to know her and learn from her, I must try to understand the things that are closest to her heart.

While it's not really an issue if Denise happens to like one type of chocolate and me another (she likes pretty much all types of chocolate, actually), it *is* a major problem if I have no appreciation for those key passions and issues that define her life. She would feel I didn't "get her."

So if God says He loves Israel with an everlasting love and that Israel is the apple of His eye, how does He feel when we display no interest or affection for Israel? How does He feel about the church being entirely indifferent to this deep passion of His?

Let's go one step further. How might God feel about His body and bride, the church, moving beyond indifference into actually *persecuting* the Jewish people whom He loves?

Denise has an overwhelming compassion for children, especially those who are deprived or in particular need. Seeing reports on TV or hearing stories about children suffering will often move her to tears. Our relationship would be much less profound if I were indifferent to this.

If we don't know someone's passions, we cannot properly understand their feelings and thoughts. We will be oblivious to their dreams and even misrepresent them to other people.

As Christians, we say we want to know God more, yet our traditions make us blind to this whole area of His heart—an area He says is vital for Him. Again and again in His Word, as we have seen, God makes it clear that He loves Israel, the Jewish people, passionately and with an "everlasting love." If we want to know Him more, then we must ask Him to show us His heart in this area so we can share His passion for the Jewish people.

The church is to be the expression of God's heart throughout the earth. We are His bride, but also His body. We must carry His heart and express His love on the earth.

We know we should love people and especially take actions to meet the needs of widows, orphans, and the poor. Why? Because *He* does. The Bible shows us that it's central to God's heart!

Why do we struggle so much to love Israel as God says He does, then?

I believe the answer is that our tradition tells us that God has finished with Israel, and if that is the case why would He still have any affection for her? He has surely "moved on"!

This tradition, as we shall see, is based on an incorrect premise—that God has rejected Israel and, further, that the church has replaced Israel. So let's examine these common church fallacies.

CHAPTER 9

THE CHURCH HASN'T REPLACED ISRAEL

Most of us have inherited a picture that looks something like this: the Jewish people had their chance, received a covenant from God called the "Old Covenant," then blew it and were rejected by God. Now it's the church's turn, and God is only interested in the church, with whom He has made the New Covenant. All God's plans, purposes, and blessings have now transferred to the church, while only the curses remain for the Jews.

This picture has come through religious tradition, but is it really what the Bible tells us, and is it what Jesus and His followers believed?

In Genesis 17:7 and onward, God proclaims that He has made an *everlasting covenant with Abraham's descendants.* The sign of this is to be circumcision. God repeats these promises to Isaac in Genesis 26:23-24, and to Jacob in Genesis 28:10-15.

Psalm 132:13-14 says that God has "chosen Zion; for He has desired it for His dwelling place: 'This is My resting place forever.'"

In First Chronicles 16:7 and Jeremiah, the words "everlasting covenant" are again used *in relation to Israel.* In Jeremiah 32:40, God reaffirms that covenant, specifically in the context of His never turning away from Israel *after* the New Covenant has been established.

God speaks again and again of an *everlasting covenant* with Israel, yet church tradition tells us that God's interest in Israel has finished, so which is correct?

The Lord says in Isaiah 59:20-21, "The Redeemer will come to Zion [Israel], and to those who turn from transgression in Jacob...from this time and forevermore."

In Romans, Paul examines the very question we are considering. "Has God cast away His people?" he asks, regarding the Jewish people. He answers the question himself—"Certainly not!" Then he reminds his readers that he is a Jewish man, and says that of course God could not reject "His own people, whom he chose from the very beginning" (Rom. 11:1-2 NLT).

Paul explains that, as always, there are those among Israel who have truly given themselves to God and entered into the promises offered by Him. Likewise, there are those who have not. Throughout Israel's story, there are those who accepted the things God was doing and those who did not. While all formed physical Israel, not all gave themselves fully to the truth of what this meant—walking in a faithful relationship with God. Therefore, he says, only those who are both Abraham's physical and spiritual descendants are the true Israel.

He reminds his readers that those who have entered in have done so not by their good works but by God's kindness, likening it to when God said to Elijah, "I have 7,000 others who have never bowed down to Baal" (Rom. 11:4 NLT). *God always finds a remnant who are faithful to Him.*

This was true in the days of Elijah, he says, and is still true today in the New Covenant. Some believe and are faithful to what God is doing, while others are not. Indeed, the 7,000 God mentions to Elijah are less than the number of those early Jewish believers who ultimately received Jesus as their Jewish Messiah.

So we must ask the question, *if God didn't reject Israel in the time of Elijah, would He in the time of His Messiah's reign?*

The Gentiles' Relationship to Israel

If God has not rejected them, *what then is the church's relationship to His people, Israel?* Paul goes on to explain this very clearly.

First, in Romans 11:11, he says, "They [i.e. many of the Jews] were disobedient, so God made salvation available to the Gentiles" (NLT). He explains this process in more detail from verse 17 onward using a simple picture. He likens Israel to an olive tree, which is often a symbol for the Jewish people in the Bible. He says,

> *Some of these branches from Abraham's tree... have been broken off. And you Gentiles, who were branches from a wild olive tree, have been grafted in.* ***So now you also receive the blessing God has promised Abraham and his children,*** *sharing in the rich nourishment from the root of God's special olive tree* (NLT).

I said earlier that, always, when God speaks about the Gentiles, words such as "also" and "until" appear. *We have arrived finally at the essence of these "alsos" and "untils,"* for these words, small as they are, hold the key. In Chapter 11 we will look at *until*, but first we must understand the significance of *also*.

When the New Testament talks about the relationship of the Gentiles to the Jews, it never uses the word "instead"; it is always "also." "Salvation has come to the Gentiles *also*," or, "the Gentiles partake of the blessings *also*."

There is not, then, as our tradition tells us, a tree that was the Jewish people with their covenants, which is now dead, and a new tree called the church, which has replaced the first. Instead, *there is only one tree, whose roots are the covenants made with the Jewish people, into which the Gentiles have been grafted*, or joined, through the breaking off of some (note, not all) of those natural branches.

Although this is the clearest place in which Paul deals with this matter, it is by no means the only time he does. In Romans 3:3-4, he says something similar: "What if some did not believe? Will their unbelief make the faithfulness of God without effect? Certainly not!"

Writing to the church in Ephesus, Paul explains the same principle. He tells the Gentiles to remember that they were once,

> *Without Christ, being aliens from the commonwealth of Israel and strangers from the covenants of promise, having no hope and without God in the world. But now in Christ Jesus you who once were far off have been brought near by the blood of Christ* (Ephesians 2:12-13).

"Brought near" to what? To all the things he has just listed. You have been brought near to the commonwealth of Israel and covenants of promise, and through these you have been brought into relationship with God.

We cannot have Christ without having these things then! Romans 9:4 says that to the Jewish people "pertain the adoption, the glory, the covenants, the giving of the law, the service of God, and the promises."

Note, this is all *present tense*. Paul is not saying this *used* to be true; he is saying it is true *at the time of his writing, after* the New Covenant has been entered into.

There is a parallel in what was called the British Commonwealth (now just called "the Commonwealth"). These are the countries, formerly part of the British Empire, who are still linked together in a type of union. Even though the member states are considered equal, the head of the whole commonwealth is the Queen of the United Kingdom. This union grew out of the relationships (for better or worse) between the other countries and Britain. But the Queen cannot be head of the Commonwealth unless she is first the Queen of the United Kingdom.

In the same way, *unless Jesus is still the King of the Jews and Israel, He cannot be King of this commonwealth of Israel to which we have now been joined.* The Greek word *politeia* carries the sense of citizenship, that the Gentiles have become citizens of a community from which they were distant and where they previously had no rights.

With Whom Was the New Covenant Made?

One key to understanding this principle is to go back to the question, *with whom was the New Covenant initially made?* We know it is available for all who are willing, Jew or Gentile, but our tradition tells us it was made with "the church."

However, this is incorrect in the way we understand it. In Jeremiah 31:31-34, we see the right answer:

> *Behold, the days are coming, says the Lord, when I will make a new covenant with the house of Israel and with the house of Judah—not according to the covenant that I made with their fathers.... But this is the covenant that I will make with the house of Israel after those days, says the Lord: I will put My law in their minds, and write it on their hearts, and I will be their God, and they shall be My people. ... They shall all know Me, from the least of them to the greatest of them, says the Lord. For I will forgive their iniquity, and their sin I will remember no more.*

This is a perfect description of what can only be the New Covenant that we now experience. It is also referred to in Ezekiel, in passages referenced in the New Testament.

The new covenant, then, was made with "the house of Israel." Otherwise, it's not new; it's completely different! *It is a new covenant offered first to the same people as the previous covenant was offered to.* Jesus Himself, describing His earthly mission, said He was sent to "the lost sheep of the House of Israel," not to the Gentiles (Matt. 10:6).

Paul goes on to explain in Romans what the situation exactly is for the Gentiles, using the olive tree image described above. This makes perfect sense of what we have seen already. He says the Gentiles are *grafted in* to all this through the New Covenant. This is the mystery he refers to in Romans 11:25 that he wants us to understand—what was meant originally as a New Covenant for the house of Israel was *extended to the Gentiles also.*

I used to work as a child-protection social worker. Sometimes, in extreme cases, I had to deal with adoptions. The process Paul describes is very like an adoption—loving parent(s) offer to provide a new life and family for children who are unloved and uncared for. Branches from another family tree, if you like, who would otherwise be lost.

If the parents are good adopters, the adopted child has all the same rights, privileges, and inheritance as the natural child. The parents will fully love their adopted child. But that doesn't mean they *replace* the natural child, however wayward or difficult that child may be!

Paul is at pains to say that only *some* branches were broken off. Moreover, he says that, although God made room for the Gentiles through the disobedience of some of the natural children, He wants us to have a right attitude toward those natural children, who are, at this time, "broken off" from the tree.

We will look at this more later, but that attitude could best be summed up by two words—*gratitude and honor.* "Do not boast against the natural branches," he says. How would parents want their adopted children to behave and feel in relation to their natural children, even those who were wayward?

It is like the analogy of the banquet that Jesus gave in a parable. The invited guests failed to come, so, instead, the master told the servants to invite all and sundry. In terms of the Jews, we know that some accepted the invitation and many did not—in particular, the key spiritual leaders of the nation. This allowed the invitation to be extended to the Gentiles. It is foolish, though, to think that being added to the guest list on a last-minute invitation makes you the guest of honor!

When we allow God to REWIRE our thinking—to replace our traditions with a more accurate picture—then the way we see our relationship with the Jewish people will begin to change.

Soon we will move into the final part of our examination of this area and look at the implications of all this for the future of Israel, the Jewish people, and the church. Before we do, however, we must deal with another issue or tradition that has caused tremendous damage over the centuries. It has caused the church to misrepresent God and also done massive damage to its relationship with the Jewish people.

This is the question of whether or not God is punishing Israel.

CHAPTER 10

God Is Not Punishing Israel

I grew up in Camden Town, in central north London. I walked to school down a road called Camden Road. It was a large main road, and at the top, around the corner from our house, there was a Jewish school called JFS, the Jewish Free School (which has now moved elsewhere).

One day, I was walking along and noticed a shadow descend over me. I looked up (I was about ten, maybe younger, and particularly small as a child). Standing there, blocking my path, were two enormously tall skinheads in Dr. Marten lace-ups and full skinhead outfits. One of them had a swastika tattooed on his forehead, and tattoos of a similar nature on his cheeks and knuckles (that dragged on the ground—just kidding). The other one was similar.

As they towered over me and looked down, the first one asked, "Are you *Jewish*?" in a menacing tone.

Now, I was young, but this seemed to me, even at that age, to be a particularly loaded question. I looked at the Nazi tattoos, thought for a second, and then decided that, on balance, I was probably not Jewish at that moment.

"No," I said simply. They did a double take, looked a bit nonplussed, but made way as I carried on walking. "You guys may be violent Nazis," I thought, "but you sure are dumb!"

Funny though this story may be, this kind of anti-Semitism (hatred of the Jews) has so often been birthed in and promoted openly by the church in its history. Jewish people have been tortured and killed, their synagogues and property attacked and destroyed, and all in the name of this "Christ"—the Jewish Messiah on whose salvation we depend. When it has been others attacking Jewish people, the church as a whole has mostly done very little to stand up for their "beloved" brothers and sisters, from whom they have received everything.

For much of the last 2,000 years, the church has said that God wants to punish the Jewish people for supposedly killing Jesus and has called the Jewish people cursed and offensive for this reason. Those who have killed Jews in the name of Jesus have often done so on the basis of their belief that God hates the Jewish people and is punishing them for crucifying Jesus. If God hates them and is punishing them, it is only a logical step to say that we are doing God's will if we punish them for Him. Often, it is as if the church has even set itself up as God's instrument of revenge and coercion. In the Spanish Inquisition, Jews were tortured and forced to renounce their faith and embrace Christianity.

Time and again, Jews have been attacked and hounded from their communities, expelled from countries, and blamed for every evil under the sun. Vicious lies have been propagated about them and used as justification for violence and oppression. My own family came to Britain at the turn of the century, at a time when many Jews sought refuge from attacks (called *pogroms*) that were happening across much of the former Russian Empire.

My mother always told me that her parents' families had originated in an area called Bessarabia, which is currently Moldova/Ukraine. I was aware that they had left because of persecution.

When researching this book, I came across this chilling quote regarding the Kishinev pogrom of Easter, 1903. The quote is from the *New York Times*, straight after the event:

> The anti-Jewish riots in Kishinev, Bessarabia, are worse than the censor will permit to publish. There was a well laid-out plan for the general massacre of Jews on the day following the Orthodox Easter. The mob was led by priests, and the general cry, "Kill the Jews," was taken up all over the city. The Jews were taken wholly unaware and were slaughtered like sheep. The dead number 120 [Note: the actual number of dead was 47/48 and the injured about 500]. The scenes of horror attending this massacre are beyond description. Babies were literally torn to pieces by the frenzied and bloodthirsty mob. The local police made no attempt to check the reign of terror. At sunset the streets were

> piled with corpses and wounded. Those who could make their escape fled in terror, and the city is now practically deserted of Jews.[1]

It is chilling to read that Christian *priests* led the persecution against my ancestors that probably caused them to flee to England.

Centuries before this, however, there had been much persecution of the Jews in England itself. In 1190, 100 Jews were massacred in York for no other reason than that they were Jewish, and after more persecution, in 1290, King Edward finally expelled all the Jews from England, an edict not officially undone until 1655.

A papal decree of 1218 led many European nations, including England, to enforce the wearing of a symbol marking Jews out, as a sign of social stigma. At times, they were able to pay extortionate sums for the privilege of *not* wearing this, until it became compulsory.

Most people are aware of and appalled by the yellow stars the Nazis forced Jewish people to wear. What they're not usually aware of is that the Nazis didn't initiate but *resurrected* this humiliation, which originated in the church of Jesus the Jew.

Although the reasons for all of this are complex, key among them is this idea that God Himself hates the Jewish people and wants to punish them for what they did to Jesus. Supposedly, they are a cursed people. Christians have often, therefore, felt that persecuting the Jews was partnering with God's business. Much has been made of the need to not be contaminated by the Jewish people's supposed degeneracy.

Martin Luther, that great initiator of the Protestant Reformation, wrote a treatise called *The Jews and Their Lies*. This illustrates and sums up Christian anti-Semitism.

He stated, "You cannot learn anything from them except how to misunderstand the divine commandments," and, "for us Christians they stand as a terrifying example of God's wrath."

He went on to write, "Then eject them forever from this country. For, as we have heard, God's anger with them is so intense that gentle mercy will only tend to make them worse and worse, while sharp mercy will reform them but little. Therefore, in any case, away with them!"

The church, then, according to Luther, is to understand how much God hates the Jews, and to do God's work in ensuring His vengeance and hatred is enacted against them.

He then suggested the following plan of action:

> First to set fire to their synagogues or schools and to bury and cover with dirt whatever will not burn....
>
> Second, I advise that their houses also be razed and destroyed. For they pursue in them the same aims as in their synagogues. Instead they might be lodged under a roof or in a barn, like the gypsies....
>
> Third, I advise that all their prayer books and Talmudic writings, in which such idolatry, lies, cursing and blasphemy are taught, be taken from them....

> Fourth, I advise that their rabbis be forbidden to teach henceforth on pain of loss of life and limb....
>
> Fifth, I advise that safe conduct on the highways be abolished completely for the Jews....
>
> Sixth, I advise that usury be prohibited to them, and that all cash and treasure of silver and gold be taken from them and put aside for safekeeping....
>
> Seventh, I commend putting a flail, an ax, a hoe, a spade, a distaff, or a spindle into the hands of young, strong Jews and Jewesses and letting them earn their bread in the sweat of their brow, as was imposed on the children of Adam....[2]

This horrifying blueprint for persecution has been enacted through the centuries against the Jewish people, often, but not exclusively, in the name of Yeshua, their King.

It is awful to see that the plan of action suggested by Luther sounds like a detailed instruction guide for the Nazi Holocaust. Travel to Auschwitz and you will see a clear picture of what it looks like for Jews to be housed "in a barn," their synagogues burned and their belongings stolen, as they are made to work as a punishment and slowly exterminated.

The hatred so eloquently expressed by the founder of our Protestant Reformation, found full expression in Hitler's program. Some Nazi leaders, including Hitler, would reference or quote Luther to back up their virulent hatred of and program against the Jews.

Luther's writings on the Jews also had a negative influence on some of the German church leaders' perspectives on the Holocaust, contributing to the church's, on the whole, woefully inadequate response (clearly, there were many individual exceptions).

Little wonder, then, that Jewish people do not rush to embrace this Jesus who seems to hate them so much and call for their destruction and persecution. This is the hurdle placed before them.

Today we are seeing a disturbing rise of attacks on synagogues, anti-Semitic rhetoric, and hate crimes against Jewish people from a range of sources. Yet we have just seen that God clearly states over and again that He *loves* Israel and *yearns* for them to come back to Him. Time and again He pronounces judgment on those who would seek to attack the people He calls "My people." He is equally harsh on Israel's enemies even when He says He has used their attacks to help bring His people Israel back to Him.

We have seen, moreover, that the whole context of Jesus' life and teaching was Jewish, and that He still identifies Himself as Jewish, even at the end of time. Is Jesus Himself to be hated by God the Father for eternity? For if the Jews are hated, how much more their King and His leaders?

We have seen how His body on the earth, the church, which carried on His ministry, was initially purely composed of Jews. We would have no Gospel and no New Testament without the Jews, and no concept or understanding of God's commandments or promises.

Let's add to this that Jesus Himself asked His Father to forgive those who crucified Him; plus, in Romans, it clearly states that it was some of the Romans and some of the Jews who together put Jesus to death. Does God also hate all Romans and by extension all Gentiles? If so, this God, whose very definition is love, must hate and want to punish everyone!

I think it's more accurate to look at it this way: was the father punishing the prodigal son when he left home and ended up a slave feeding pigs? Not at all! The son simply walked out of the blessings of his father's house and into a lifestyle disconnected from those blessings.

Was the father punishing the elder son, who had been legalistically working like a servant for his father, but also stepped outside of the blessings of the father's house? Likewise, not at all! He ran to meet the prodigal and also came out to plead with the elder son.

In the same way, most of the Jewish people are walking, I believe, outside of the fullness of the Father's plans for them—outside of the reconciliation and intimacy with God that is available through their Messiah and King. But God is not *punishing* them. He is longing for them to come back into His house, to receive the fullness of His blessings. Longing even as He continues to welcome and adopt all those other sons and daughters into His home.

Now that we have established this truth, that God is not punishing Israel, we must return to the question of how God really feels about Israel, for not only does the Bible tell us that God chose, called, and loves Israel, but also it tells us that He has not yet finished with her.

NOTES

1. "Jewish Massacre Denounced," *New York Times*, April 28, 1903.

2. Martin Luther, qtd. in "Anti-Semitism: Martin Luther: 'The Jews & Their Lies'" Jewish Virtual Library, accessed December 01, 2016, http://www.jewishvirtuallibrary.org/jsource/anti-semitism/Luther_on_Jews.html.

UNDERSTANDING GOD'S PLAN FOR ISRAEL

The very title of this chapter would create a dispute in many, if not most, churches. "Surely," they would say, "God no longer has plans for Israel, only the church?" We have already looked at this mindset called replacement theology.

A key verse in this respect is Galatians 6:15-16. This is translated very differently depending on the authors of the translation. For instance, in the New King James Version it reads:

> *For in Christ Jesus neither circumcision nor uncircumcision avails anything, but a new creation. And as many as walk according to this rule, peace and mercy be upon them, and upon the Israel of God.*

Yet in the New Living Translation it reads:

> *It doesn't matter whether we have been circumcised or not. What counts is whether we have been transformed into a new creation. May God's peace and mercy be upon all who live by this principle; they are the new people of God.*

Notice just how different they are. In the first translation, the idea is that our right standing in Christ isn't determined by circumcision or affected by a lack of it. In the second, the sense is that circumcision has become completely irrelevant, and this is backed up by the translation of verse 16, which seems to suggest that God has one new people who are not interested in Jewish things such as this.

In fact, this verse is a key one many Christians have used to say that the church is "the new Israel," but it does not say that.

The first translation of this verse actually *counters* that argument and strengthens the idea of a distinct Jewish group of followers of Jesus. The "Israel of God" is identified as distinct from the Gentile believers to whom the letter was primarily addressed. In that case, Paul is actually using this phrase to specifically describe the *Jewish believers*.

The authors of the New Living Translation (a translation that is generally beautifully written) have taken a theological position that seems to contradict the very thing Paul is saying, and this has actually been the prevailing thought in the church.

When we look through that distorted lens, we see everything that is happening in the world in relation only to the church. Yet God in fact says He rules all the nations and specifically says much prophetically about the nation of Israel, just as He does about the future of the church. The two are inextricably linked.

This doesn't mean, as some people have mistakenly said, that Jewish people do not need Jesus. He's their Messiah. Of course they do! It means simply that God is still concerned with them as individuals but also as a people group.

God Hasn't Finished With Israel

One of our specialties as Christians is to take a verse that seems attractive out of context and to apply it to ourselves. In this way, we create new traditions and truths that suit us, or we apply half-truths while ignoring the other half that we are less interested in. Often, this is because it makes us feel uncomfortable.

A perfect example of this is Romans 11:29: "The gifts and the calling of God are irrevocable," or, as the New Living Translation puts it, "For God's gifts and his call can never be withdrawn."

This verse has often been used to emphasize how, even when we fail in areas that God has called us to, His plans for us remain the same. This is true because if it is a true statement about God in general, then we can expect it to be true regarding our lives.

However, the context of the verse reveals the *key* truth Paul is trying to explain. This verse forms part of Paul's explanation of the mystery of how Gentiles came to be one with Jews in the New Covenant—how you were included and brought into the covenant God had with the Jewish people He calls His own, so that you *also* became His.

Paul states that the "blindness in part" that has come to Israel will only last until the full number of Gentiles has come into the kingdom (see Rom. 11:25). He reminds the Romans that God's new covenant to take away sins is made with Israel (see Rom. 11:26-27). He then tells the Romans that the gifts and call that God has given the Jewish people can never be withdrawn (see Rom. 11:28).

So that verse in context is really about how *God still has the same call, purpose, and plan for the Jewish people and Israel.* He has *not* simply left them to their fate, says Paul, nor will He *ever.*

We know that God still has a plan for Israel from the last exchange recorded between Jesus and His disciples. In Acts 1, the author tells us that Jesus taught the disciples at different times over a 40-day period after His resurrection. Luke says that He taught them "about the Kingdom of God."

Finally, we read that when they were with Jesus toward the very end of this period, they asked Him a question: "Will You at this time restore the kingdom to Israel?" (Acts 1:6). They asked this in response to His teaching, and His comment that they should wait in Jerusalem for the coming of the Holy Spirit. They saw all this as somehow connected to the restoration of the kingdom to Israel. This is because, time and again in the Torah, these things are indeed linked.

For instance, they would have had Joel in mind. Joel 2 talks about the coming of the Holy Spirit on "all flesh," followed by great signs and wonders in the earth, and "whoever calls on the name of the Lord shall be saved. For in Mount Zion and in Jerusalem there shall be deliverance" (Joel 2:32).

So when they asked Jesus, "Will You at this time restore the kingdom to Israel?" it was not that they misunderstood His teaching, nor had they missed the point. They are not asking *whether* but *when* it is going to happen. This is clear because Jesus doesn't say, "You fools! You've got the wrong end of the stick," although this is often how people interpret His response.

He actually says, "It's not for you to know times and seasons which the Father has put in His own authority. But you shall receive power when the Holy Spirit has come upon you; and you shall be witnesses to Me in Jerusalem, and in all Judea and Samaria, and to the end of the earth" (Acts 1:7-8).

Imagine I am your boss, and we have agreed to have lunch. Later you ask, "What time are we having lunch?" and I reply, "Listen, I can't tell you what time we're having lunch yet, but please finish the work I asked you to do for now!" Does this mean we're having lunch or not? Unless I am cruel and deceitful, it means we are, but I don't know the time yet and don't want you to focus on that.

In the same way, Jesus affirms that there *is* a plan to restore the kingdom to Israel, but tells His disciples to focus meanwhile on the task they have been assigned—to be His witnesses throughout the earth.

Therefore, from this alone we know that there is still a plan for Israel. Jesus Himself said just before His crucifixion that "Jerusalem will be trampled...*until the times of the Gentiles are fulfilled*" (Luke 21:24). Again, we see that word "until" used in regard to the Gentiles and Israel.

So if there is a plan, then what is it?

GOD PROMISED TO RESTORE THE PEOPLE TO THE LAND

We can get so caught up in politics that we miss what God is doing in the world. Yet God always moves through people to accomplish His plans.

The Bible is full of threats from God to scatter the Jewish people throughout the world if they walked out of relationship with Him and forgot their covenant with Him. The last of these came from Jesus Himself. As He drew near to Jerusalem, He began weeping. He said of the city,

> *For days will come upon you when your enemies will build an embankment around you, surround you and close you in on every side, and level you, and your children within you, to the ground; and they will not leave in you one stone upon another, because you did not know the time of your visitation* (Luke 19:43-44).

Alongside these threats, however, there is *always* a promise that eventually God Himself will cause the Jewish people to come back to their own land, including a promise from Jesus Himself. Those little words appear time and again—*until* and *also*—small words with huge importance.

Where God's promises to Israel are eternal, His threats are time limited. Not just because Israel will come back to Him, but because *He Himself* will initiate something; He will Himself draw them back to the land He has promised them.

In Jeremiah 23:7-8, God talks about a time, after the Messiah has come I believe, when people will say, "As the Lord lives who brought up and led the descendants of the house of Israel from the north country and from all the countries where I had driven them."

In Jeremiah 32, God has this to say:

> *I will certainly bring my people back again from all the countries where I will scatter them in my fury. I will bring them back to this very city and let them live in peace and safety. They will be my people, and I will be their God. And I will give them one heart and one purpose: to worship me forever, for their own good and for the good of all their descendants. And I will make an everlasting covenant with them: I will never stop doing good for them. I will put a desire in their hearts to worship me, and they will never leave me. I will find joy doing good for them and will faithfully and wholeheartedly replant them in this land* (Jeremiah 32:37-41 NLT).

There's a key point here, which God repeats. Many Christians think the Jews will become believers in Jesus and then go back to Israel. Yet the Bible says precisely the *opposite*. In Ezekiel 36:23-28, for example, it says that God will draw them back to their land, and *then* He will sprinkle clean water on them and give them new hearts of flesh for their hearts of stone.

This is precisely what we see today. God has drawn more than six million Jewish people back to Israel, but only now are we beginning to see the start of them turning to their Messiah. There are more believers in Israel today than ever before—more fellowships springing up across the nation. God is doing something.

In Zechariah, it talks about the "spirit of grace and supplication" being poured out on Israel, and the people turning to their Messiah. I believe this turning has begun and will accelerate.

There is something else, too—*time and again the return of the Jewish people is linked to the land flourishing again.* Israel is the only nation that has had a net gain of trees in the last hundred years. Much of the land that was swamps and marshes is now fruitful, fertile agricultural land.

The prophet Amos talked about impending judgment coming on Israel, but also how all nations would be shaken. He then talked about how God would restore the house of David, so that all the Gentiles who were His would be included in His blessings. In the final verses of his prophecy, however, he talked about this restoration of Israel:

> *"I will bring my exiled people of Israel back from distant lands, and they will rebuild their ruined cities and live in them again. They will plant vineyards and gardens; they will eat their crops and drink their wine. I will firmly plant them there in their own land. They will never again be uprooted from the land I have given them," says the Lord your God* (Amos 9:14-15 NLT).

Clearly, the issue of the land is contentious in modern political discourse. There are so many opinions, so many rights and responsibilities that need to be negotiated. This is not about entering the political debate or justifying any kind of oppression or injustice where it might exist. As followers of Jesus and as Jews, we are called to demonstrate God's love to all people, for we are called to represent

Him on the earth. And God's love, as Jesus demonstrated, is always radical, powerful, and surprising. It often leads us to acts that seem counter cultural and even folly to others—such as talking to a woman from Samaria who would normally be off-limits for a Jewish man, or refusing to condone the actions of religious leaders who wanted to stone a woman, or dying on a Roman cross when He could have saved Himself.

However, this *is* about starting with an understanding of what the Bible says and what it specifically tells us about God's purposes and plans regarding Israel. If we look at this, the pattern is clear.

The Land in the Covenants

Genesis 13:14-17 says:

> *After Lot had gone, the Lord said to Abram, "Look as far as you can see in every direction—north and south, east and west. I am giving all this land, as far as you can see, to you and your descendants as a permanent possession. And I will give you so many descendants that, like the dust of the earth, they cannot be counted. Go and walk through the land in every direction, for I am giving it to you"* (NLT).

And Genesis 17:7-8 says:

> *I will confirm my covenant with you and your descendants after you, from generation to generation. This is the everlasting covenant: I will always be your God and the God of your*

> *descendants after you. And I will give the entire land of Canaan, where you now live as a foreigner, to you and your descendants. It will be their possession forever, and I will be their God* (NLT).

God tells Abraham that the sign of this covenant between Him and them will be the circumcision of all the males. In verse 13, God says, "Your bodies will bear the mark of my everlasting covenant" (NLT).

God then changes Abraham's wife's name from Sarai to Sarah, as a sign that she will have a son who will carry the covenant. Abraham is dumbfounded because Sarai is so old. He mistakenly says, "May Ishmael live under your special blessing" (Gen. 17:18 NLT). God corrects Abraham:

> *But God replied, "No—Sarah, your wife, will give birth to a son for you. You will name him Isaac, and I will confirm my covenant with him and his descendants as an everlasting covenant. As for Ishmael, I will bless him also, just as you have asked. I will make him extremely fruitful and multiply his descendants. He will become the father of twelve princes, and I will make him a great nation. But my covenant will be confirmed with Isaac, who will be born to you and Sarah about this time next year." When God had finished speaking, he left Abraham* (Genesis 17:19-22 NLT).

In case there is any confusion about who these descendants are, God clearly states that the covenant will be passed to and through Isaac. He corrects Abraham, and once He has finished He leaves, as though to say, "This is My last word. No more discussion on the matter!"

Unfortunately, although God gave a clear and direct word, there has since been *great deal* of discussion on the matter. Mostly this has been people wishing to reverse or undermine God's covenant with the Jewish people and the land.

Note that, although God promises to bless Ishmael and his descendants too, He clearly says that His covenant with the land of Israel—the covenant that will be a blessing to the whole world—is to pass to Isaac and his descendants.

So He loves and blesses all people, but has a special plan and purpose for Isaac's descendants and for their location in a specific place.

In Psalm 105:8-11, the author spells out clearly God's position:

> *He always stands by His covenant—the commitment He made to a thousand generations. This is the covenant He made with Abraham and the oath He swore to Isaac. He confirmed it to Jacob as a decree, and to the people of Israel as a never-ending covenant: "I will give you the land of Canaan as your special possession"* (NLT).

We have already seen that in Jeremiah, as well as numerous other places in the Bible, God reaffirms that His covenant with the Jewish people cannot be nullified and will be fulfilled one way or another. He is faithful when we are faithless. His call is without repentance and stands despite our, and specifically Israel's, disobedience.

In Romans, we have seen that Paul, the apostle to the Gentiles, says that the covenants *still belong to the Jewish people.* We are grafted in to those that are relevant to us. Yet nowhere does Paul say that the land part of God's covenants is done away with. Indeed, *Jesus makes clear that the restoration of Israel is part of God's agenda, but in the Father's timing.*

Much of the confusion stems from the idea of covenants, plural. Many Christians forget that the New Covenant has not replaced all of God's covenants; it is more specifically about defining how we obtain righteousness with God. It doesn't replace all the covenants God made with the people of Israel, or else Paul would not be speaking of them as belonging to the Jewish people in the present tense. He is still called the God of Abraham, Isaac, and Jacob. If these covenants were all done away with, this title would be pretty redundant and misleading.

This is worth exploring in a little more depth, for we must be very clear about it.

"MY PEOPLE"

It is very interesting that the Bible states that *every people group, every nation, and every individual belongs to God. And yet He calls Israel "My people."* He repeats it over and over again in case anyone should miss or misinterpret it.

When God sent Moses to Pharaoh, He told him it was "that you may bring *My people,* the children of Israel, out of Egypt" (Exod. 3:10). God told Samuel to anoint Saul as "commander over *My people* Israel, that he may save *My people* from the hand of the Philistines" (1 Sam. 9:16). God told David that, "You shall shepherd *My people* Israel, and be ruler over *My people* Israel" (1 Chron. 11:2).

Matthew quotes this same phrase when he speaks of the prophecies regarding Jesus: "But you, Bethlehem, in the land of Judah, are not the least among the rulers of Judah; for out of you shall come a Ruler who will shepherd My people Israel" (Matt. 2:6). So we see that God specifically claims the people of Israel as *His* people, *even when He appoints leaders to lead them.*

Indeed, it was never God's intention for them to have kings. Their uniqueness as a people stemmed from the very fact that they were led and governed directly by God Himself.

When they clamored for a king, God finally allowed it, but ultimately used this for His plan to restore His *direct* lordship of His people through the Messiah, the Son of David.

"MY LAND"

Similarly, the Bible also says that the whole world was made by and belongs to God. Psalm 24:1 says, "The earth is the Lord's, and all its fullness, the world and those who dwell therein"—*yet God calls this one place, this tiny strip of land we call Israel* (actually a rather bigger strip, but we'll leave that for now), *"My land."*

God makes it clear time and again that although He has given the whole earth to man, He has reserved this one people and this one patch of land for the fulfillment of His purposes.

For instance, in Jeremiah 2:7, God chastises His people Israel: "I brought you into a bountiful country, to eat its fruit and its goodness. But when you entered, you defiled *My land* and made My heritage an abomination." He repeats this in Jeremiah 16:18.

In Ezekiel 36:5, God says, "Surely I have spoken in My burning jealousy against the rest of the nations and against all Edom, who gave *My land* to themselves as a possession, with wholehearted joy and spiteful minds, in order to plunder its open country."

In Ezekiel 38:16, we see that even when God allows or causes others to conquer it, as a consequence of the sins of His people, He still calls it "My land." Joel 1:6 says, "For a nation has come up against *My land*, strong, and without number."

No matter what, God still calls it "My land."

"MY HOLY MOUNTAIN"

Finally, we see something else. *Even within Israel, God narrows it down and repeatedly describes Jerusalem as "My holy mountain." So, although He has narrowed our focus from the whole world and told us that Israel is His land, He says that Jerusalem, even out of this land, is specifically His—holy and set apart for His purposes.*

For example, in Isaiah 66:20: "'Then they shall bring all your brethren for an offering to the Lord out of all nations, on horses and in chariots and in litters, on mules and on camels, to *My holy mountain* Jerusalem,' says the Lord." *Holy* means "set apart" for God's purposes.

Zion is another name used for Jerusalem. "Blow the trumpet in Zion, and sound an alarm in *My holy mountain!*" (Joel 2:1).

Ultimately, we know it was here that Jesus was crucified, redeeming His people and all people. Jerusalem is indeed set apart for the holiest of all God's purposes on the earth. *Yet God never renounces His claim to Jerusalem. And why would He? He says He is coming back to rule there, after all.*

One way or another, we see again and again that God uses Israel and the Jewish people to fulfill His purposes on the earth and to demonstrate His power and glory. They are like His "touchstone."

There is a parallel that takes us back to the story in Genesis of the Garden of Eden. God gives the whole garden to mankind but says there is this one thing, this tree of the knowledge of good and evil, that they cannot eat from. But mankind could not resist.

So it is with Israel. God says, "Take dominion over all the earth, but this one people and their land belong to Me!" Yet the nations cannot resist touching and taking that which God says belongs only to Him.

We need to be clear: God does not condone poor or unjust behavior from the Jewish people in the land. Indeed, *He sets a very high standard for them, far higher than He expects of the nations around them.* For example, they are to treat the stranger in their land as their own; to operate justly; and to look after the poor, widows, and orphans specifically, from whatever race or creed.

Time and again God brings His people back not to religious ritual, but to issues of their hearts and their love of justice and mercy. In short, He brings them back to the two core commands—love God, and love your neighbor as yourself.

So to say that the land belongs to the Jewish people and vice versa is not to give *carte blanche* to Israel to do whatever they like. Quite the opposite. As I said, God sets a *higher* standard of how to treat others for Israel, as His people—His examples.

Rather like the world expects Christians to live out a higher standard of behavior and love than the average person, so it often feels like the world expects Israel to live out a higher standard of righteousness, justice, and charity than any other nation.

Though you would probably not know it from the reported news, Israel in many ways does live up to this. It is the only true democracy in the Middle East. It is in Israel, in contrast to the countries all around it, that all people (not just Jews) are free to practice the faith of their choice without fear; are able to vote and participate in all aspects of life, regardless of ethnicity, religion, or gender; are free from persecution in regards to their sexuality; and have those core freedoms, protections, and rights we experience in the West.

In other ways it falls short, as all nations do. Israel has been surrounded, since its inception as a modern nation in 1948, by nations that primarily wish for and in many cases openly talk about its destruction rather than seeking good relations, and when we look at Israel we need to understand this context. Israel has had to fight many wars simply to maintain its existence as a nation.

However, this is not the right book to examine all the historical rights and wrongs, nor to discuss the politics and all that goes along with that. Rather, we must at least start with the right premise in relation to the Bible—that God gave the land to the Jewish people and vice versa—certainly if we are to impose God's standards on them. At the very least this must mean we acknowledge Israel's right to exist as a nation!

Now, however, as we reflect on God's purposes, we will see two things: first, that in God's timescale Israel becomes even *more* important as the course of history unfolds, and second, that Israel's restoration is a blessing for the whole world.

CHAPTER 12

ISRAEL'S RESTORATION

In everything, the pattern we repeatedly see is "to the Jew first; then to the Gentile." Paul says in Romans 2:9-11 (NLT): "There will be trouble and calamity for everyone who keeps on doing what is evil—for the Jew first and also for the Gentile. But there will be glory and honor and peace from God for all who do good—for the Jew first and also for the Gentile. For God does not show favoritism."

So there is no favoritism, but *there is distinction.* Israel and the Jewish people are like a time clock. *What happens with them prefigures what will happen to the rest of the world, so the events the Bible predicts for them are of monumental importance for us all.*

AS HISTORY UNFOLDS, ISRAEL IS KEY

I am not obsessed with end-times theology and speculation. I just thought I had better be clear about that, because there are a lot of people who are, often at the expense of their actual lifestyle. I have no desire or inclination to be like that. Life is way too challenging and too complicated to get obsessed with minute details of the future and speculations that take our minds off what God requires from us, and others need, in the here and now. That stuff is more than enough of a struggle for me.

However, the cure for misuse of something is not disuse but *correct* use. We must focus on how to live in the here and now, but we can't just ignore what the Bible has to tell us about God's promises and plans for the future, and Jesus Himself made some startling remarks in this respect. Toward the end of His time with the disciples, for instance, He spoke of what was to come for the Jewish people and Jerusalem. He said that the Temple and Jerusalem would be destroyed. He continued:

> *They* [the Jewish people] *will be killed by the sword and sent away as captives to all the nations of the world. And Jerusalem will be trampled down by the Gentiles* ***until*** *the period of the Gentiles comes to an end* (Luke 21:24 NLT).

The first part of this has been fulfilled. Jerusalem was destroyed by the Romans in AD 70 and the Temple destroyed completely. A subsequent revolt led by Bar Kokhba from AD 132-136 was crushed by the Roman Emperor Hadrian. Vast numbers of Jews were killed—580,000, according to Cassius Dio. Others were sold into slavery. To add insult to injury, Hadrian renamed the land "Syria Palestina" (from which the name "Palestine" is derived) after the greatest enemy of the Jews, the

Philistines. The aim of this was to erase all connection of the Jewish people to their homeland.

From this point on (in addition to the previous Babylonian and Assyrian exiles, and some voluntary emigration to other countries), most of the Jewish people were to be found dispersed around the nations of the world. This is known to Jewish people as the *Diaspora*.

But what does the second part of what Jesus is saying mean—"until the period of the Gentiles comes to an end"? Jesus tells them that something else is still to come, but what? If we do not know, we may miss it. Perhaps it has even begun already, before our eyes.

Often we just ignore these kinds of awkward comments. I have a friend who has a special ability to say, when situations are clearly awkward, "Awkward!" in a seriously loud voice, thereby rendering the situation yet more awkward. Perhaps it's time we did that, for we usually need to feel awkward and uncomfortable before we're willing to question our assumptions and examine the issues we've ignored.

We cannot ignore this "until"; instead we need to look at Jesus' prophecy in the context of other biblical prophecies. We will look at just two here, out of many.

In Zechariah 12 the prophet talks about a time to come for the nation of Israel. In this passage he says:

> *This message concerning the fate of Israel came from the Lord: "This message is from the Lord, who stretched out the heavens, laid the foundations of the earth, and formed the human spirit. I will make Jerusalem like an intoxicating drink that makes the nearby nations stagger when they*

> *send their armies to besiege Jerusalem and Judah. On that day I will make Jerusalem an immovable rock. All the nations will gather against it to try to move it, but they will only hurt themselves"* (Zechariah 12:1-3 NLT).

This continues a little further on:

> *Then I will pour out a spirit of grace and prayer on the family of David and on the people of Jerusalem. They will look on me whom they have pierced and mourn for him as for an only son. They will grieve bitterly for him as for a firstborn son who has died* (Zechariah 12:10 NLT).

How can we know this has not been fulfilled yet? First, we need to understand that prophecy works on different levels. This means that each prophecy may have more than one fulfillment. For instance, Jesus said that Elijah would come before the end times, as prophesied, but also that he *had* already come, in the form of John the Baptist who carried the same spirit as Elijah. In a similar way, Paul talks about many antichrists coming before the final figure known as *the* Antichrist. Many of the prophecies concerning Jesus also had previous "fulfillments." So this prophecy, too, may be partly fulfilled but still not truly fulfilled. This is contrary to our Western way of thinking but not to a truly Jewish, biblical mindset.

Second, Zechariah says that after all these things have taken place and God has fought on behalf of Israel, He will pour out a "spirit of grace and prayer (supplication)" on the Jewish people, looking to the One whom they have pierced and mourning for Him as an only son. This was yet to happen, for the One they pierced is Jesus Himself, and He was yet to be pierced at this point.

Zechariah also says that Jerusalem will become a very heavy stone and a cup of reeling for all the nations around, and that all who try to lift it will, literally, be ruptured (or get a hernia!). This is like reading current affairs—it is precisely what we see today.

Let's look at one more Scripture:

> *For behold, in those days and at that time, when I bring back the captives of Judah and Jerusalem, I will also gather all nations, and bring them down to the Valley of Jehoshaphat; and I will enter into judgment with them there on account of My people, My heritage Israel, whom they have scattered among the nations; they have also divided up My land* (Joel 3:1-2).

God says He Himself will judge the nations that have divided up His land (note that He again calls it *"My land"* here), for which He is massively displeased, to say the least.

Again, how do we know that this is an event to come? Because, before he says this, Joel prophesies regarding the outpouring of God's Spirit that was to come. And Joel 2:28-32 is the passage that Peter quoted on the day of Pentecost, to explain to the people in Jerusalem what was happening when the Holy Spirit was poured out on the disciples.

So the judgment that Joel is referring to must come after the Holy Spirit has been poured out, but also after the Jewish people have been scattered and the land divided up by the nations. This scattering is also precisely what Jesus predicted would happen and which reached its height after AD 135.

We see a clear picture here: God Himself is displeased with the nations for their actions. As history unfolds, God says He will bring them into judgment, even as He will restore Israel. This seems to correspond to what Jesus meant when He said, "Jerusalem will be trampled until the period of the Gentiles comes to an end."

Another confirmation of this is that both Old and New Testaments indicate that Jesus will return to Jerusalem. A little after the passage we looked at in Zechariah, the prophet says that in the time when all the nations gather against Jerusalem, "His feet will stand on the Mount of Olives" (Zech. 14:4). He talks about how "the Lord shall be King over all the earth" (Zech. 14:9), and Jerusalem will be safe forever after.

When the disciples saw Jesus ascend to heaven from the Mount of Olives, it says that two white-robed men suddenly stood among them (see Acts 1:10-11). These men assured the apostles that Jesus would return from heaven "in the same way you saw Him go!" The disciples would have been reminded of those words of Zechariah.

Israel's Restoration Is Blessing for the Whole World

It is not all bad news, however! In Romans 11:12, Paul says something amazing to his readers. Speaking of the Jewish people, he says, "Now if their fall is riches for the world, and their failure riches for the Gentiles, how much more their fullness!"

Or in the New Living Translation: "Now if the Gentiles were enriched because the people of Israel turned down God's offer of salvation, think how much greater a blessing the world will share when they finally accept it."

The fact that *some* Jewish branches were broken off from the natural olive tree is what allowed God to perform this miracle of grafting *Gentiles* into the Jewish tree. This despite them being "wild" olives, not seemingly of the same species as the natural (Jewish) olive!

This breaking was therefore an amazing blessing to the Gentiles. They have been brought into all the covenants, as we have seen, and now have all the same *benefits*, the same *identity*, and the same *purpose and call* as the Jewish people.

But Paul says there is an even bigger blessing coming to the whole world when the Jewish people, or natural olive branches, are grafted back into their own tree and into this New Covenant through the blood of Jesus, their Messiah.

Paul describes this as "life from the dead." It is as if the natural order of things will be restored. Israel will be able to fully enter into her call and purpose as God's true representative on the earth. The older sons and daughters will come back into the house and delight fully in the love and forgiveness of their King and Savior.

This does not mean that the Gentiles will cease to be His ambassadors; it's simply that the picture will be *complete*. Israel will be restored. Until this, all is not quite right and the world cannot experience the fullest expression of God's blessings.

Perhaps we can think of it like a marriage where only one partner truly loves God. They can serve God, serve those around them, and be a good witness to their spouse, yet only when their partner comes fully into a relationship with God can the marriage be truly in spiritual unity and the grace on them as a couple multiplied because of that.

The Gentile church and Jewish believers are in a marriage together. This is the one new man. Not a Gentile, but a true marriage of the two—a miracle and mystery performed by God.

Another way to look at this is Paul's description of how "the root supports the branches," referring to the Jewish people as the root. As the Jewish people come back into their family and are one with the adopted children, all working for the Father's purposes, so the root becomes healthy and strong, and the family of God becomes more complete. In this we see a movement toward the fulfillment of God's purposes for mankind, to at last have a people for Himself.

The church has for too long skipped over the importance of this "even greater blessing," this "life from the dead," and therefore failed to take its role in the fulfillment of these plans seriously. Yet it is always the role of God's people to partner with His purposes on the earth to see them fulfilled rather than simply watch them happening like indifferent spectators. As the apostle James says, once we have "heard" we must "do" or else our faith is dead!

So we must ask, what are the implications of all we have looked at for individual followers of Jesus and for the church as a whole? What should our response be to all this? And what difference does this make for the Jewish people themselves?

It is not enough to simply REWIRE our thoughts because, to paraphrase James—REWIRED thinking and feeling must lead to REWIRED actions.

Conclusion: God Cares about Our Attitudes and Actions in Relation to Israel

The church must be aligned with God's heart and purposes, and by the church I mean you and me and every person who calls themselves a Christian, a believer, a follower of Jesus, or any other name they want to give themselves. To properly reconnect with God's truths is to reconnect with His heart.

Although not universally embraced, it is not always that contentious to reconnect with the truth about the Jewish Jesus and His followers. People are often interested and excited, especially when they start to see how it brings Jesus alive to them more and helps them understand the New Testament more fully.

It is far more contentious to reconnect with the truth about God's heart for Israel. Yet time and again, as we have seen, God makes it clear that He cares hugely about our attitudes and actions toward the Jewish people and the nation of Israel. He also makes it clear that for Him these two are inextricably linked.

So when God said to Abraham, "Those who bless you I will bless, those who curse you I will curse," He meant it, and as He never nullifies it or takes it back, He still means it (see Gen 12:3).

When God says in Joel that He will bring the nations into judgment for dividing up what He calls His land

and for mistreating what He calls His people, He means this also.

When the psalmist declares that we should "Pray for the peace of Jerusalem," this is God's word to us (Ps. 122:6).

God calls the children of Israel "the apple of His eye"—something that is precious to Him, not because of any inherent goodness in them, but because of His choosing and investment (see Deut. 32:10; Zech. 2:8).

So, when we pray for the restoration of Israel and the Jewish people, and pray for them to come to know their Messiah, we are not pursuing a side interest. When we pray for them to be grafted back into their own olive tree and experience the intimacy with God that we experience, *we are praying in line with the very heart and purposes of God.* We are praying for the greater thing that Paul talked about to happen, the process that is like "life from the dead," which he says will be even more amazing than the joining of the Gentiles to God's covenants and to His covenant people.

When we allow God to show us a more accurate picture of Jesus and of His heart for Israel, we begin to help undo the misperceptions and misconceptions that the church has propagated about the Jewish Messiah and His "church" (really, the word *ekklesia* that Jesus uses just means a group of people who are "called out" and brought together).

The return of Jesus is linked to the restoration of Israel, so we are also actually praying for the very thing we crave. Jesus Himself said to the Jewish people in Jerusalem, "You shall not see Me until the time comes when you say,

'Blessed is He who comes in the name of the Lord'" (Luke 13:35). So, in praying for the Jewish people to know their Messiah, we are hastening the return of Jesus.

In Isaiah 49:1-6, there is an amazing passage describing the Messiah's anointing and ministry. Verses 5 and 6 (NLT) say the following:

> *And now the Lord speaks—the one who formed me in my mother's womb to be his servant, who commissioned me to bring Israel back to him. The Lord has honored me, and my God has given me strength. He says, "You will do more than restore the people of Israel to me. I will make you a light to the Gentiles, and you will bring my salvation to the ends of the earth."*

Only Jesus has brought light to the Gentiles and God's salvation to the ends of the earth! But Isaiah speaks of *three* key things the Messiah will do—bring light to the Gentiles, bring salvation to the ends of the earth, *and restore the house of Israel.* The church has typically missed the third and concentrated on the other two.

I believe that, because of this, the church has missed out on a key part of the heart and call of Jesus to His own natural brothers and sisters, the Jews. Paul says that even if they are "enemies" when they oppose the Gospel, we should love them for all that has come to the Gentiles through their forefathers. Without the Jewish people, we would have no Bible, no covenants to be a part of, and no Messiah. Truly, we are all indebted to them.

We have seen that the church has often been the biggest persecutor of the Jews and one of the greatest sources of anti-Semitism on the earth. In doing so, she has been cursing her roots. How can she be a fully healthy tree while doing this?

It is time for us to stand up and declare that enough is enough! Once we have this understanding, we must rise up and bless our Jewish brothers and sisters, *demonstrating* God's love to them—the love of their own Messiah and King.

We must strive to live out the most accurate representation of God's heart on the earth. How else will we make them jealous in a way that causes them to want what we have? (Or indeed anyone else, for that matter?)

It is not sufficient to simply ignore this. There is no neutral ground in God's order. When we are simply indifferent, we are missing both a part of God's heart and some of the blessings that come from acting in obedience to it.

Paul actually says that it's not enough to receive the benefits of the covenants we have been brought into. In Romans 15:27, he says, "For if the Gentiles have been partakers of their spiritual things, their duty is also to minister to them in material things."

This principle still applies if we wish to step into the fullness of the blessings God has for our lives and for our churches. I believe we must find ways to bless the Jewish people and the nation of Israel.

The prophet Isaiah declared, "For Zion's sake I will not keep silent, for Jerusalem's sake I will not remain quiet, till her vindication shines out like the dawn, her salvation like a blazing torch" (Isa. 62:1 NIV).

To not remain silent means that we need to speak about the truths we've looked at concerning who Jesus really is and concerning God's heart and plans for Israel. We must do this even when all other voices seem to state the opposite. When others try to divorce Jesus from His Jewish identity and to deny God's love and plans for Israel, we must be willing to speak and stand up for what we believe to be the truth.

To not be silent even means finding ways to materially bless the Jewish people where they are in need. There are many needs, both in Israel and for Jewish people in other parts of the world, toward which we can contribute. In doing this, we both demonstrate God's enduring love for them as a people and show them the way in which the blessings of God overflow through our relationship with their King.

One way Paul suggested we can do this is by blessing the *believers* who are Jews, in Israel and elsewhere. This both acknowledges the debt we have and contributes to the spiritual awakening of God's people, Israel. For these Jewish believers can be a blessing and witness of the truth about Yeshua to their own people in ways that we cannot.

By doing this, we also start to take responsibility for undoing some of the damage done in the name of their Messiah, who is also our Messiah, by our spiritual ancestors. When we allow our thinking to be REWIRED and restore the Jewish lens, then we can effectively start to *re-present* Jesus, the Jewish king, to His own people. Whilst every person has to decide what to make of the claims of Jesus and His followers, my concern is that Jewish people should be able to make this decision at least based on an accurate picture rather than the distorted one with which they have been presented.

As we begin to do this and as more and more Jewish people start to reconnect for themselves with the truth about their Messiah, we need to go further and wrestle with the same questions that Paul and the other apostles all had to wrestle with: *what does it mean for Jew and Gentile to live as one in the body of Christ*?

In Part Three, we will reconnect with the truth about God's design for the church. Now that we have seen that the church hasn't replaced Israel, what exactly should this marriage between Jews and Gentiles look like? What can this teach us about how to live out our faith today?

In answering these questions, we will start to answer the most vital question that follows on from Parts One and Two: how do we practically restore the Jewish lens to the church?

PART THREE

IMPLICATIONS FOR THE CHURCH

CHAPTER 13

RESTORING THE BALANCE

The application of the Jewish lens is liberating but also poses new challenges and questions for us. Once we've seen how Jesus and the early disciples lived, thought, and taught as Jews, how do we apply this to our faith to more effectively build the kingdom of God, serve our generation, and live authentically ourselves?

In short, how much are Gentiles supposed to live as Jews, and how much are Jews supposed to live as Gentiles?

I believe that so much more of the New Testament deals with these issues than we realize. The apostles and the early church community had to wrestle with this because it was a brand-new challenge for them—where before there had been one people, there were suddenly two joined together.

It is only once we have restored the Jewish framework for understanding Jesus and the early church that we can fully understand the issues they were addressing in the New

Testament. Once we do restore it, however, I believe that lines of detail will reappear that will give us a fuller picture of God's blueprint for our lives and for the church community as a whole.

People have looked at similar issues over the centuries, often in much greater detail than I have, and generally this has been a great blessing to the church. Unfortunately, between the ideas and the implementation, things can go wrong.

Often what happens is like a pendulum swinging one way and then back the other. Maybe you have seen this in church life. One moment the focus is on evangelism, and it seems all that matters is reaching new people and introducing them to God. Then we remember we're supposed to build a community for people to join, so the focus switches to that instead.

One moment everyone is focused on encountering God, the next we remember that we need to make sure we're being relevant to people who don't know Him. And so, each time, instead of building on what has gone before we end up lurching from one thing to another, trying to correct things as we go. Like a beginner riding a bicycle, once you lose your balance it's hard to get it back because you end up overcorrecting.

It can be just like this with what we have looked at so far. The church (and specifically church leaders) has made terrible errors in denying and destroying its Jewish roots. Yet those attempting to restore this aspect of our faith to the church have at times made errors too.

At one extreme, we have Christians who would rewrite history and the Bible to deny or diminish the very

Jewishness of Jesus, to strip away or spiritualize all references to Israel, and to simply ignore the truths we have looked at in Parts One and Two.

At the other extreme, there are those who have placed an overemphasis on particular aspects of restoring the Jewish culture. This can be equally unbiblical and unhelpful, especially if it becomes more about tradition for tradition's sake than about enhancing our capacity to become like Jesus. In the same way that the biggest obstacle to the Jewish people recognizing Jesus as their Messiah has often been Christians and the church, the biggest obstacle to Christians recognizing God's truth about the Jewish people and Israel has often been the people who have already had this revelation.

Denise was recently cooking a pasta sauce that required a little chili zing. She's a fantastic cook, but she was tired and in a hurry, and her tendency in that case is to follow the recipe a little slavishly. So, when she came to the bit that told her to add two teaspoons of chili flakes, she did exactly that and thought no more of it.

Unfortunately, chili flakes vary a lot in how hot they are. When we came to taste the dish, the chili had turned it so ferociously hot that neither of us could stand it. I like spicy dishes more than Denise, but even I couldn't really stomach it. Instead, I used it as a chili sauce on other dishes for the next week! The chili had totally overwhelmed all the other flavors.

When it comes to the "Jewishness" of our faith, what we want to do is add the flavor and spice without overpowering the other ingredients. We're not looking to follow the letter of the law but to make the perfect dish.

Where initially some Jews tried to make Gentiles become Jewish and later Gentiles tried to make Jews become like Gentiles, I believe it's time for us to find the right balance so we can cycle together in the direction God has for us without toppling over. As we do this, it will be a great blessing to us all and help us contribute to the journey described at the end of Part Two—because if we haven't integrated these truths into our lives and communities, how can we effectively play our role in blessing the Jewish people?

A New Community

What we therefore need to do is restore our picture of how Jews and Gentiles lived together in the early church communities. *The key principle we must understand as we go on this journey is this: if God has brought Jew and Gentile together into one community, they must be better together than either one on their own.*

The Jewish people were not an accident that God would rather forget. The Gentile people are not second best or an afterthought. Together, this new community must be better, not worse, than what has come before, for God always transforms things "from glory to glory." Moreover, in many places in the Old Testament, as we have seen, God spoke through His prophets about a time when He would gather together the Gentiles with His Jewish people and make them into one community.

When I married Denise, I initially thought there were ways in which if she would only think and act and feel like me everything would be all right. Especially in situations where conflict arose, each of us would wonder why the other responded so differently to the way they should have.

As time went on, we began to appreciate something. First, we each had a unique background that caused us to behave and think in certain ways. Second, some of our differences were caused by the fact that we are, er, different! God has not called us together so that Denise can become identical to me or me to her. He has given us to each other precisely so that our differences would become a blessing to both of us. So that we can learn together. Third, through the differences in our characters, backgrounds, and ways of thinking, we learn principles that help us grow as individuals and as a family.

We are, in short, better together than apart. We learn, we grow, we face challenges, we navigate conflict, and in all of it we become the people God has called us to be.

I might have wondered initially why Denise felt that piles of paper stacked everywhere was not a good filing system, and Denise may have wondered why I felt the need to play guitar till late into the night. But, over time, I learned to let her help me with filing systems, and she learned to give me an office and shut the door! We learned principles that we can only really learn in this way—by living together.

So it is with Jews and Gentiles. But we can only experience these things if we are willing to walk together and ask the right questions. The kinds of questions we need to ask are:

- What should this new community look like?

- How do the two people groups live together harmoniously?
- What principles can we learn from this process?

Fortunately, there's someone we can turn to for expert guidance, and that is Paul, the apostle formerly known as Saul.

From Saul to Paul

Once the church's biggest persecutor, Paul became the greatest architect of these new communities involving both Jews and Gentiles across the world. He wrote more than two thirds of the New Testament and, as such, is its most important author. Yet perhaps he is also its most misunderstood. As the key builder of the early church movement outside of Jerusalem and Israel, he specifically refers to himself as an "apostle to the Gentiles [non-Jews]."

As we have seen, however, he also held fast to his Jewish framework for living and went to great lengths to demonstrate that he was doing so. We saw that even Paul's trial and death were a result of him doing this very thing—trying to demonstrate publicly that he didn't teach Jewish people to disobey the commandments of the Torah.

Although he was sent to the Gentiles, the Bible says it was his custom to go first to the synagogue in any city, where the Jews met, and only afterward take the Gospel to the non-Jewish community. As the key apostle and builder of these new communities, Paul needed more than anyone to answer this key question—*how do Jews and Gentiles live together in the church?*

He addressed issues relating to this question many times in his letters to the new churches, which we read in the New Testament. Although much of what he said can seem complex and, as Peter said, "hard to understand," I believe that it is not impossible for us to find the keys we need if we will simply REWIRE our thinking, restore the context, and allow the text to speak to us.

Paul was raised as a strictly observant Jew, living according to the commands that the children of Israel had inherited. Not only that, but he studied under a famous rabbi called Gamaliel and was clearly a gifted and well-thought-of student—when the first martyr, Stephen, was stoned, it says that the people laid their clothes at the feet of, as he was then, "a young man called Saul."

This doesn't mean that he was the hat-check guy! It means that Saul was the one who approved of the killing, and that he was proactively leading the persecution of the early church under the authority of the chief religious leaders. As Paul puts it himself in his letter to the Galatian churches:

> *For you have heard of my former conduct in Judaism, how I persecuted the church of God beyond measure and tried to destroy it. And I advanced in Judaism beyond many of my contemporaries in my own nation, being more exceedingly zealous for the traditions of my fathers* (Galatians 1:13-14).

Shortly after this incident, though, Saul had his dramatic encounter with Jesus on the road to Damascus. Temporarily blinded, he was led to a house there, where for three days he didn't eat or drink.

At the same time, Jesus spoke to a man called Ananias and told him to go and lay hands on this man, who had been persecuting the church! Answering Ananias' protests, Jesus told him:

> *Go, for Saul is my chosen instrument to take my message to the Gentiles and to kings, as well as to the people of Israel. And I will show him how much he must suffer for my name's sake* (Acts 9:15-16 NLT).

Jesus tells Ananias that Paul's mission will be primarily targeted at reaching the Gentiles, incorporating them into the new church, and reaching even those with great influence. Yet also he will be sent to the "people of Israel." It is one of the very few times that the Jews are referred to as the "also" because the pioneering aspect of Paul's ministry will be to those who currently have no connection to the Hebrew God and His commandments.

As well as this, Jesus tells Ananias that this whole work will not be easy. Paul will have to suffer in the process of his mission to both the Gentiles and the Jews. And so it proved to be. Paul faced opposition and attacks from every side—first from Jewish religious leaders, who saw Paul as undermining their traditions and leading Jews into a new, sacrilegious cult; second from Gentiles, for apparently undermining their *own* gods and foisting this Jewish one on them; and finally from within the church itself.

Time and again, Paul had to face challenges from the people he was supposed to be working with and for. These challenges came from both Jew and Gentile, and from leaders and followers. At one point, Paul even had to stand up to Peter and some of the other apostles.

Wherever Paul went, he would establish new communities of believers, each part of the growing *ekklesia*, or church. As Paul's mission was to both Jews and Gentiles, these churches consisted of two previously separate peoples learning how to live together in one new community.

Having birthed these communities with the aid of other disciples such as Barnabas, Paul then established leaders before moving on. He later wrote to them to advise, admonish, encourage, and instruct them on how to develop their faith and their communities according to God's blueprint.

Jews and Gentiles had lived both *separately* and *differently* before coming together in these churches, so many of the issues Paul had to address related to this new challenge—*how do we do this together?* It was completely new territory for everyone.

So in Paul's letters to the Philippians, Ephesians, Colossians, Thessalonians—again and again he addressed problems and controversies arising in the new communities.

Traditionally, when it comes to the subject in hand, the church has interpreted Paul's argument as being this: the "Jewish thing" is, at best, irrelevant and, at worst, a hindrance. However, we have already seen that this is far from the truth, and if we look more closely I suggest that a different picture emerges. *Fundamentally, Paul is concerned with keeping the flock together.*

GOD'S SHEEPDOG

If Jesus is the great shepherd, as He said, then Paul is like His sheepdog, going from one side of the flock to the other to ensure that no one gets off track and is dragged away from the truth.

One moment he is on one side, calling back those who are overemphasizing the need for everyone to follow Jewish traditions, and the next he is on the other side, rebuking those Gentiles who are ignoring God's commandments and heading off into immoral living. He is always looking both at the present community and ahead to ensure that the flock is moving in the right direction—like any good sheepdog, listening to the voice of his master!

The chief place that he does this is in the longest letter of all—his letter to the church in Rome. That letter contains *five key principles* that I want to bring out to show us how to integrate the truths from Parts One and Two into our lives and our churches.

Notice that I am saying *principles.* Often we want a very black-and-white direction—should we do this or that? *Just tell me what to do!* Like the woman at the well of Samaria, we want Jesus to clarify exact details of our type of worship, our celebrations, our eating habits, et cetera.

Instead of discussing those details with her, Jesus brought her back to the more important truths, which start in the *heart.* The rest, He said, is just that—details. Get the principles right first.

Likewise, in this area I believe the key is not so much in the outward *form* of our actions as the heart motives behind them. The principles I want to bring out, therefore, aren't rules. You cannot plug in the questions and get the answers. It is always dangerous when we seek easy answers to complex questions—answers that require no thought, reflection, or study on our part. That kind of dogmatic thinking doesn't reflect a relationship but a type of religion in the negative sense. It creates restrictive practices, judgmental thinking, and the categorization of people and behaviors as "in" or "out."

It also doesn't really represent a Jewish, and therefore biblical, way of thinking. The framework Jesus taught in was one where discussion was central, questions were encouraged, and each disciple was expected to wrestle with Scripture and with his own heart.

In Judaism, there is an understanding that each generation must seek God's wisdom in applying the principles and commandments in Scripture to their generation and culture. The work of rabbis and their disciples was to wrestle with the correct application of what we call the Old Testament to present-day living. This is what Paul meant when he said to Timothy: "Be diligent to present yourself approved to God, a worker who does not need to be ashamed, rightly dividing the word of truth" (2 Tim. 2:15). Timothy only had the same Scriptures as the rabbis—the ones that Paul calls the "word of truth."

Likewise, Paul said, "Work out your own salvation with fear and trembling" (Phil. 2:12). In that light, I want to encourage you to consider these principles. I believe they will keep us on the right track to restoring this marriage between Jews and Gentiles. I also believe it was God's intention that these principles should inform how we live as individuals and as church communities more widely. They are part of what we can learn that makes us better together.

With that in mind, let's take a look at what Paul says in Romans, as well as some of the other letters he wrote to the churches.

Paul's Letter to the Romans

The first key to understanding these principles is to ask *why Paul wrote such an enormously long letter to the church in Rome.* It is so much longer than most of his other letters. In fact, Romans is the longest letter we know of in the ancient world!

It was written in a time when composing, recording, and sending a letter was a far more complicated affair than it is today. None of this just clicking "send" on an e-mail, or even licking a stamp. A scribe would generally do the actual writing, while the author worked on the letter itself, perhaps with the help of others. The composition and recording itself might take weeks.

Then there was the delivery—perilous journeys across vast areas of land, at risk from bandits, the elements...it was no Amazon Prime.

All this means that, in composing such a long letter, Paul had some serious things to say.

To understand his purpose in writing this specific letter at this particular time, we must understand what was going on in the Roman church that was troubling Paul. For a more detailed account of the historical context of these issues, I would suggest reading David Pawson's section on Romans in his book *Israel in the New Testament*. I will just summarize the pattern he describes here.[1]

Pawson explains that the church in Rome had been through four distinct phases up to this point. First, there was a beginning sometime after the Day of Pentecost. In Acts we're told that Jews from many parts of the ancient world were in Jerusalem listening, and that some 3,000 became followers of Jesus on that very day.

It says in Acts 2:10 that some of those who heard Peter's message on the Day of Pentecost were from Rome, both Jews and converts to Judaism. So it is highly probable that the church in Rome was initially composed of believing Jews.

In the second phase, those Jews would have evangelized in Rome, leading to the church becoming a mix of both Jewish and Gentile believers. However, around the AD 50s, the emperor, Claudius, banished all Jews from Rome. This is recorded in Acts 18:1-2:

> *Then Paul left Athens and went to Corinth. There he became acquainted with a Jew named Aquila, born in Pontus, who had recently arrived from Italy with his wife, Priscilla. They had left Italy when Claudius Caesar deported all Jews from Rome* (NLT).

This was the third phase of the Roman church—when it was composed entirely of *Gentile* believers.

Finally, in the AD 60s, Emperor Nero invited the Jews back into Rome, and so the issue arose—would the Gentile believers welcome the Jews back into their fellowship?

It seems that problems arose as a result of this, leading to a potentially dangerous split in the church in this key location. So Paul, like a good sheepdog, wrote to counter it, to keep the flock together.

Unlike the other churches Paul wrote to, however, he had not founded this Roman church or appointed its leaders. Moreover, at this point he had never even been to Rome. He says in the first part of his letter,

> *One of the things I always pray for is the opportunity, God willing, to come at last to see you. For I long to visit you so I can bring you some spiritual gift that will help you grow strong in the Lord. When we get together, I want to encourage you in your faith, but I also want to be encouraged by yours.*
>
> *I want you to know, dear brothers and sisters, that I planned many times to visit you, but I was prevented until now. I want to work among you and see spiritual fruit, just as I have seen among other Gentiles. For I have a great sense of obligation to people in both the civilized world and the rest of the world, to the educated and uneducated alike. So I am eager to come to you in Rome, too, to preach the Good News* (Romans 1:10-15 NLT).

Paul starts by saying how much he wants to visit them, to encourage them and teach them about God's truths. For now, however, he will have to make do with this letter.

This means that, because he doesn't know them yet nor they him, he must first establish his credentials. He is talking as an apostle but not as their spiritual father, so he must tread more gently than he does in his letters to the churches who knew and accepted him already as their leader and instructor. Therefore, he takes his time building his arguments before he really addresses the key issues.

We saw that Paul's fundamental point is in Romans 11. There he addresses that key question, *has God rejected his people Israel?* and he answers himself, in the strongest terms: "Certainly not!" He wants the readers to be clear about this vital issue that he has been leading up to.

The idea growing in the minds of Gentile believers, that God has abandoned Israel and the Jews, has led to the beginnings of a split in the Roman church. In the process of addressing it, Paul painstakingly lays out the key principles by which Jew and Gentile can live together in one community, according to God's order, and in a healthy, mutually beneficial manner.

Paul's very purpose, as we shall see, is not simply to counter this divisive idea of a split, but to prevent the church from making precisely the kind of errors that came to afflict it in the centuries that followed.

In his letter to the Ephesians, Paul says that, through Christ, God has made of Jew and Gentile "one new man," where previously there was a division and conflict. In his letter to the Romans, he explains how this one new man must operate.

I believe that when we lost sight of these principles in relation to Jewish and Gentile peoples worshiping together, we fundamentally lost sight of them for the church as a whole. So when we recover them in this context we recover them for the church as a whole, too, and bring healing to the wider church community.

In the remaining five chapters we will look at five principles that Paul addresses to Jewish and Gentile believers in his letter to the Romans, and consider how we can apply these to our lives and churches today. As well as showing us how to live together as Jewish and Gentile believers, these five principles give us a framework for how to restore the Jewish lens we have been talking about in practice.

The first principle, and the foundation for the others, is humility.

NOTE

1. David Pawson, *Israel in the New Testament* (Ashford: Anchor Recordings, 2014), Chapter 3.

Principle 1: Humility

Humility is a fundamental requirement for walking with God. Several times the Bible says that "God resists the proud, but gives grace to the humble," so we miss this at our peril (James 4:6).

In a marriage, it is vital that each person approaches the other with this humility, otherwise the marriage is headed for the rocks. As Jews and Gentiles have been made one in Jesus, humility lays the groundwork for everything else.

So Paul addresses both Jews and Gentiles with this fundamental instruction—"Don't boast!"

Paul's Instructions to the Jews

He speaks first to the Jews about this and tells them, "Don't boast in the law" (or Torah):

> *You who call yourselves Jews are relying on God's law, and you boast about your special*

> *relationship with him. You know what he wants; you know what is right because you have been taught his law. You are convinced that you are a guide for the blind and a light for people who are lost in darkness. You think you can instruct the ignorant and teach children the ways of God. For you are certain that God's law gives you complete knowledge and truth* (Romans 2:17-20 NLT).

> *Can we boast, then, that we have done anything to be accepted by God? No, because our acquittal is not based on obeying the law. It is based on faith. So we are made right with God through faith and not by obeying the law. After all, is God the God of the Jews only? Isn't he also the God of the Gentiles? Of course he is* (Romans 3:27-29 NLT).

Paul tells the Jewish believers not to boast in the fact that they were the ones who had God's commandments in the form of the Torah. He says, "You boast in them but *you can't even keep them!*" He also says, "They don't actually save you; rather, the fact that you are unable to keep them, *even though they are good*, leads you to understand your need for a Savior." Therefore, God's mercy (our "acquittal") is obtained not by obeying the commandments in the Torah but by placing faith in what God has done through the death of Jesus on our behalf.

He also says, "Don't boast that you're the ones able to teach everyone about God's ways simply because you have the Torah." He reminds them that the key to understanding

God's commandments, and therefore teaching others about them, is a reformed heart that's functioning in line with God's. It is *how* you live out the commandments that matters.

Jesus addressed this again and again with the Jewish religious leaders. His criticisms were the same—you think you can be righteous by following rules, but your heart attitude is wrong and you're misleading others, too. Here, Paul is addressing that same religious pride among Jewish believers.

I find it interesting that Christians, at times, talk to me as if I have a secret, esoteric knowledge through being a Jew brought up with some knowledge of the Old Testament. If only this were true. However, I have also experienced a certain tendency among some in the Messianic community (Jewish believers) and among some Gentile believers who have found an understanding of the Jewish framework for their faith. They begin to elevate the Torah and God's commandments above Christ. Paul, however, always works the other way around—he uses the Torah to elevate Jesus.

All God's commandments, he says, point us in the direction of Christ, our need for Him, and His work in our lives. Or, as he puts it, "Christ is the end [*telos*: better translated "goal"] of the law [Torah]" (Rom. 10:4). He constantly steers the church away from the idea that external adherence to a set of rules or commandments can be central to its faith or practices. Instead, he says, our relationship with Jesus must always be at the center.

However, notice what he does *not* say—that these commandments of God are now irrelevant, obsolete, or archaic. In fact, he says the very opposite:

> *But still, the law itself is holy, and its commands are holy and right and good. ...So the trouble is not with the law, for it is spiritual and good. The trouble is with me, for I am all too human, a slave to sin* (Romans 7:12,14 NLT).
>
> *I love God's law with all my heart. But there is another power within me that is at war with my mind. This power makes me a slave to the sin that is still within me. ...So you see how it is: in my mind I really want to obey God's law, but because of my sinful nature I am a slave to sin* (Romans 7:22-25 NLT).

Remember, our word *law* is a poor translation of the word *Torah*. More accurately, we could translate it "teaching" or "instruction." Paul says that because of our weak, sinful nature, God's teaching on how to live couldn't save us. Instead, it is what God accomplished through Christ, so that "the power of the life-giving Spirit has freed you from the power of sin that leads to death" (Rom. 8:2 NLT).

We are freed from the power of sin, then. We are not freed from the Torah (teaching), as such. It would be odd for Paul to say we are liberated from God's teaching on how to live—from commands he says are "just and holy." Elsewhere, he says, "All Scripture is inspired by God and is useful to teach" (2 Tim. 3:16 NLT), and we must remember that he is referring to the only Scripture they had—the books we call the Old Testament.

We are, however, set free from all condemnation in our failure to keep God's commandments, to follow His instructions. We receive God's mercy and then the empowerment to live out a new life. We are released to live a life in relationship with the Holy Spirit. Our hearts and minds can now be led by His nature at work in us. We do not look to keep the letter of the law, nor fear condemnation for failing to keep it. We seek instead to find this goodness and to let our lives express it.

So, if we return to the teaching of Jesus we looked at earlier, we can understand what He means. The purpose of the command "do not murder" is really to teach us to love others. Therefore, to fulfill it means more than just an absence of murder. It means an absence of *hatred*. Even more, it means the *presence* of His supernatural love in our hearts. Only the Holy Spirit in our hearts can develop this sense of love and therefore enable us to fulfill the command to love others in practice.

So Paul says to the Jews, "Don't boast in the law!" The degree to which we express God's loving nature is more dictated by how much we let the Spirit control our mind, leading to life and peace (see Rom. 8:6). The Jewish people have a legacy of the Torah that can be wonderful and useful if put in its proper place and used rightly. However, it can also be a hindrance if used wrongly.

Don't think you have a monopoly on teaching about God. Have humility. Recognize that all of us Jews and Gentiles—*everyone, everywhere*—are equally sinful without Jesus. We all need Him to save us, and this must be our starting point. Only His Spirit in our hearts brings out the fullness of the commandments and empowers us to understand and live them out as His ambassadors.

I have experienced situations where it felt like Messianic Jewish believers were approaching these matters without the humility that Paul is describing. Instead, the attitude was, "Now we're back and we're gonna tell you how it really is!" as if everything the church has achieved or developed over the centuries and is accomplishing today has somehow become null and void. This is clearly nonsense.

As Jewish people who have seen and experienced the "replacement theology" we discussed earlier in the book, we must know better than to stand up and say, "We're here to *re-replace* you Gentiles." There has to be another way, and this is the humility that Paul talks about in his letter to the Romans.

It can be really easy to slip into seeking knowledge for knowledge's sake. Paul reminds us that all our understanding must help us to *live out* the mercy and grace we have received in Jesus. If this knowledge doesn't help us to develop a deeper relationship with God, it is of no use and will only do what Paul elsewhere says knowledge for knowledge's sake does—puff us up (see 1 Cor. 8:1).

Whenever this happens, the church begins to move toward a legalistic mindset where the keeping of rules becomes more important than the heart behind them. We end up exactly where the Pharisees, the religious leaders, were—the very ones who Jesus rebuked because they placed too much importance on external observance and forgot about the heart. That is not what we are trying to restore.

The purpose of the commandments is "love from a pure heart," or, as Jesus said, the summing up of the whole Torah is to love God and love our neighbors as ourselves (although we must still remember that *to sum something up is not to make it obsolete so much as to capture its essence*).

So Paul urges the Jews to approach their Gentile brothers and sisters with humility.

Paul's Instructions to the Gentiles

Having told the Jews not to boast in the Torah, *Paul turns his attention to the Gentiles and tells them also not to boast*. Using the analogy of an olive tree that we looked at in Chapter 9, he says, *"Don't boast that you are the chosen ones, but have an attitude of humility toward the Jewish people."*

> *And if some of the branches were broken off, and you, being a wild olive tree, were grafted in among them, and with them became a partaker of the root and fatness of the olive tree,* ***do not boast against the branches****. But if you do boast, remember that you do not support the root, but the root supports you* (Romans 11:17-18).

The Jews made the mistake of thinking they were "it" because they had God's covenants and commandments. Paul tells the Gentiles emphatically, *"Don't make the same mistake by thinking you're now 'it' instead of them."* This comes back to the very heart of what we looked at earlier in chapter 9, and it is a simple, stark warning.

Paul says that the Gentiles, even though they were *wild*, were brought into relationship with God as a result of *some* branches from the Jewish (olive) tree being broken off. "Don't be confused," he tells them, "and think that there is a new tree. There are not two trees, but one, and you have been made part of this Jewish olive tree by a miracle of God." So have an attitude of thankfulness for being "grafted in" and of humility toward that natural olive tree. That is what he means when he says, "*If* you do boast."

This humility must extend both to the Jews who are already believers and to those who are not yet, for if there is only one tree then there remains a special place and purpose in God's heart and plans for those original or "natural" branches—a purpose that, as we saw, will ultimately be for the blessing of all mankind.

Getting the Balance Right

The church has been plagued by this very thing that Paul is warning the Romans about. Each denomination boasts that it alone has the full revelation of God. The world looks on and sees Christians boasting against one another over who has God's ultimate revelation, whereas Paul says, "If you disagree on some point, I believe God will make it plain to you" (Phil. 3:15 NLT).

It seems so easy, when we feel we have received a revelation about something from God, to think we are now "it" and "they" are not. Every new thing God does seems to create an in crowd and an out crowd. But Paul tells us to avoid this way of thinking. Don't boast that you're "it"; instead, remain in that place of humility. The context in which Paul tells us to learn this is in our relationships as Jews and Gentiles, so we must apply it there first.

I have sometimes felt this attitude from Christians in relation to my journey as a Jewish follower of Jesus. First, there can be a sense of "Ah, yes, you've finally come to your senses!" that is more pronounced than it would be for non-Jews. It is as though each individual Jew has been willfully rejecting Jesus rather than living estranged from Him, as anyone else.

Second, because the church has taught replacement theology, when I first became a believer most Christians talked to me as if I had left one tree (Jewish) and joined a new one (Christian). This was somewhat confusing for me. It was at times more or less explicit, but the sense was that I had stopped being Jewish, in all but a nominal sense, and become a Christian.

I remember someone saying how happy I must be that I could now eat bacon! Er, that's not the greatest aspect of my salvation, actually (and I don't anyway). This was also a thought based on the idea that the old tree is irrelevant now. I was free to live without the Torah—without the "baggage" of my Jewishness, one might even say!

But the Torah is "just and holy" and "good and spiritual," as Paul says. So the issue is not to be free of God's teaching. It is from the power of sin and death that I am free! *The issue is how to live out the purpose of the Torah fully and freely, without fear of punishment and without self-righteousness.*

When Jews (or Gentiles) elevate God's commandments above Jesus, above the very One who is their "telos" or goal, they can take the church into legalism. And, like God's sheepdog, Paul tells us not to get off track and lead the flock astray in this way. He emphasizes this elsewhere, too—for instance, in his letter to the Galatians.

Here, in his letter to the Romans, Paul also reminds Gentile believers that when they boast that they are now "it" and have replaced Israel, they open the door for a break with the Jewish people and their roots that leads to error and arrogance. This causes them to stop learning from their Jewish roots and from their Jewish brothers and sisters, and it has caused huge damage to the church.

This wrong attitude is displeasing to God, who resists the proud and has commanded the Gentiles to treat the Jewish people with gratitude and love. After all, it is from them that the Gentiles have received their "Old Testament," their New Testament, and their Savior. It is through the Jews that the Gentiles have been brought into their covenant relationship with God.

Replacement theology also opens the door to a profound loss of connection with God's heart for the Jewish people and the nation of Israel. Ultimately, it has led to the church's mistreatment of the Jewish people that I referred to in earlier chapters, because if the old tree is dead and God hates it we should too. If the Jewish people are no longer special to God, then neither should they be to us. If God no longer has plans for them, then we can ignore them altogether.

We have seen what happens when the church tells the world how God is finished with the Jews and even hates them. It's time for the church—for non-Jewish followers of the Jewish King—to heed Paul's warnings and remember the tree into which they are grafted.

For Jewish followers of Jesus, it is important that we remember we have all been saved by the same grace, not by our ethnic background. We are different, but not better than one another.

With an attitude of humility established in our hearts, let's address the next principle Paul outlines—*acceptance*.

ACTION

Whether you are a Jewish or Gentile believer, approach the other with humility. Esteem them more highly than yourself. Honor them as a believer but specifically as who they are. Approach them with a heart to learn from them.

CHAPTER 15

PRINCIPLE 2: ACCEPTANCE

Having established that humility is central to the process of becoming "one new man" in Christ, Paul goes further into the practicalities of working this out together.

In the new community of believers there were those who previously had no knowledge of God's teaching in the Torah at all. Then there were the Jewish believers, who themselves had a spectrum of belief about how to follow God's commandments, just as today there are those who interpret commandments more or less strictly.

Some of these Jewish believers not only felt they had a monopoly on teaching others about God's instructions on how to live, but they also went on to judge those they felt didn't live up to their standards.

Paul says that, although the commandments themselves may be good, you can't judge those who seem on the outside to be less "holy" than you. *You can't condemn those who don't follow your interpretation of the commands.*

Ultimately, Paul says, like everything else in our walk with Jesus, faith is the determining factor. Whatever others do in terms of remembering God's traditions and following His Word, so long as they do it in faith we should not judge them according to our interpretation of how to express our relationship with Him.

Clearly, this is not about ignoring obvious breaches of God's commandments and principles that are for everyone. Paul isn't saying it's OK to commit adultery, to steal, or to make sacrifices to other gods, so long as you do it by "faith." He is talking about the specific nuances of how we choose to follow God's commandments and to express our faith through external ritual.

Jesus had spent much of His ministry addressing the Jewish religious leaders for precisely this kind of judgmental thinking and behavior. Again and again He told them, "When you judge others for how they do or don't measure up to your standard of observance, you yourselves are missing the very point of the commandments you claim to be following." Now Paul carries on where Jesus left off.

It is amazing how quickly this process happens—a new spirit or idea creates a vibrant, exciting new way of doing something. The heart of it is pure—an expression of a newfound truth or a new way to live. Then come some guidelines, necessary to describe what this new thing is and isn't. But somehow judgment always seems to creep in, and the very thing Jesus roasted the Pharisees for finds its way back into the church.

Here, Paul reminds the Romans, both Jews and Gentiles, "You all have different ways of doing this journey, of interpreting God's teaching, and living it out. So don't judge one another."

And as before, we will start with the Jews.

Paul's Instructions to the Jews

In the book of Acts, we have seen how the Jewish leaders responded to the influx of non-Jewish disciples.

> *And so my judgment is that we should not make it difficult for the Gentiles who are turning to God. Instead, we should write and tell them to abstain from eating food offered to idols, from sexual immorality, from eating the meat of strangled animals, and from consuming blood. For these laws of Moses have been preached in Jewish synagogues in every city on every Sabbath for many generations* (Acts 15:19-21 NLT).

So the decision had already been determined: *we will not try and make followers of Jesus who aren't Jewish live according to all the Torah commandments that the Jewish believers follow.* Paul, then, is reminding the church of this principle. He tells the church members to not judge one another according to their observance.

I am passionate about restoring the Jewish lens so that every believer can learn to read the Bible as a whole book, because I believe there are riches to be found for everyone in it. But this is not the same as forcing people to try and obey every detail of the commandments God gave to the Jewish people or even forcing everyone to follow one interpretation of the Bible.

Paul says to the Jewish believers, "You can follow the commandments in the way you feel is right, by faith, but don't judge the Gentiles when they don't follow them as you do." It is wrong for Jewish ministries to try to force the church back to following every detail of the Torah.

First, as Paul makes clear, no one is able to do this. Second, the church is Jew and Gentile together, and it is wrong to try to reverse the decision the apostles took in Acts.

Rabbinic Judaism has always been an evolving thing with an understanding that fresh interpretations of God's teaching must be applied to new situations. We too must allow these fresh expressions of faith to coexist and flourish together.

Sometimes it seems the most zealous people in this respect are Gentiles who rediscover the things we have discussed in Parts One and Two. They can become critical of church practices and judge people who celebrate Christmas and Easter or pay no attention to the biblical festivals, the Sabbath, and so on. To judge like this is wrong, however. These people have the freedom to celebrate as they see fit, and most Gentiles are not likely to feel comfortable trying to celebrate the biblical festivals exactly as Jewish people do.

Paul's Instructions to the Gentiles

Paul likewise tells the Gentiles not to judge the Jewish believers who choose to follow the Torah's commandments. If a Jewish believer chooses to celebrate the Jewish biblical feasts, that doesn't mean they are "returning to the law" in a negative sense.

If they were to do this to try to attain *salvation*, that would be different. However, I haven't come across any who are. Rather, they see it as a more authentic and meaningful celebration to follow the biblical feasts as they were commanded by God and to find Christ expressed in those feasts.

So, as they celebrate Passover, they understand and celebrate more fully that He is our Passover, the Lamb of God. As they celebrate the Feast of Tabernacles (*Sukkot*), they celebrate the full meaning of God coming to dwell with His people and providing for them.

The Feast of Weeks, or *Shavuot*, is also known by its Greek name, *Pentecost*. It commemorates the giving of the law by God to Israel at Sinai. In the New Testament, the Holy Spirit was poured out on those first believers on the Day of Pentecost. This demonstrates that His coming was the fulfillment of God's promises to Israel. Specifically, it fulfilled the promise in Jeremiah to "put My law in their minds, and write it on their hearts; and I will be their God, and they shall be My people" (Jer. 31:33).

Just as Jesus brought out the full meaning and purpose of God's commandments, so in Him we find the full expression and meaning of God's feasts.

So Jewish people do not need to be set free from the biblical feasts that God commanded them to celebrate! We cannot judge Jewish believers who choose to follow the Torah. Perhaps, instead, we should try to learn from them the full meaning of these feasts in Jesus.

Paul and Nuala O'Higgins state in their book *Good News in Israel's Feasts* that each of the feasts has three levels of significance/meaning:

- First, they celebrate and remember a key event in Israel's history.
- Second, they have a prophetic significance relating to the work of Jesus.
- Third, they tell us about the journey we are on ourselves as believers.[1]

Usually, we focus on the first of these three. Yet the more we understand how these feasts give us insight into what Jesus has done, is doing, and will do in our lives, the more they come alive and help us understand our journey of salvation and transformation.

However, it is one thing to suggest that Gentiles learn from the biblical feasts and another to judge them for not adopting them as their own. Paul gives us some clear guidelines on how we are to proceed in all this:

> *Let not him who eats despise him who does not eat, and let not him who does not eat judge him who eats; for God has received him. Who are you to judge another's servant? To his own master he stands or falls. ...One person esteems one day above another; another esteems every day alike. Let each be fully convinced in his own mind. He who observes the day, observes it to the Lord; and he who does not observe the day, to the Lord he does not observe it. He who eats, eats to the Lord, for he gives God thanks; and he who does not eat, to the Lord he does not eat, and gives God thanks. ...Therefore let us not judge one another anymore* (Romans 14:3-6,13).

Paul says whatever you do by faith in regard to these matters is OK. It is not so much what you choose to celebrate or the exact rituals you choose to use within that, but why and how you do it. *So let us be free to be who we are and not judge one another. Rather, let us celebrate the difference and learn from one another.*

This idea of being who we are is the next principle that we will look at.

ACTION

Celebrate and live according to your faith, but don't judge those who wish to live differently from you. Try to appreciate the different expressions of faith and ritual while holding on to the fundamentals. Do not judge those who wish to celebrate the biblical festivals, nor those who choose to celebrate modern traditions.

NOTE

1. Paul and Nuala O'Higgins, *Good News in Israel's Feasts* (Stuart, FL: Reconciliation Outreach, 1997), 12.

CHAPTER 16

PRINCIPLE 3: IDENTITY

When I first joined the church, I was already a singer-songwriter, among other things. I'd started doing gigs and I loved it. The music that had influenced me was not worship or "church" music at all, but the full spectrum of artists I had been listening to when I was younger. Once I came into the church, I soon became part of the worship team and spent many years happily involved in serving in this way.

When it came to writing songs, however, try as I might I could never seem to write songs that would work in worship. They had too many words, they seemed a bit different—they just didn't fit! In fact, often when I showed people new songs, they would say things like, "Yeah, that's good. Did you write it before you became a believer?" and I would sheepishly reply, "Er, no, I wrote it last week."

Slowly but surely, it began to dawn on me that my gift wasn't about writing church worship songs; it was writing contemporary songs from a different perspective. Once I realized this, I could stop trying to be someone I wasn't in order to fit in, and follow my own path instead. I began to record albums and publish my music the way that God intended—out in the world, instead of in the church setting.

I think the same thing happens when it comes to Jews and Gentiles in church. We have Jews trying to fit in with Gentile customs and Gentiles trying to be Jews. However, the beauty of this whole marriage is not that we become like each other; instead, it's about *diversity* and *complementarity.* If we try and become like each other, we negate that.

The Mystery of the "One New Man"

I was talking to someone recently who had been a Christian a long time. We were discussing this issue and we began talking about the verse in Paul's letter to the Galatians that says, "There is neither Jew nor Greek, there is neither slave nor free, there is neither male nor female; for you are all one in Christ Jesus" (Gal. 3:28). I asked him what he thought this meant, and he replied, "That there are no more Jews or Gentiles; we're all together in Jesus."

"OK," I said. "In that case, it makes no difference if your wife is a man or a woman—because there are no men or women, right?"

As we talked, he began to see that Paul's argument must be a bit more subtle than that. Paul is talking in the context of how we attain righteousness and saying we have all attained righteousness through Jesus. There is one route and nobody is better than another because of gender identity, ethnic background, or social status.

Paul is removing any reason for a sense of pride one over another. However, he is not obliterating distinction altogether. Elsewhere, he talks about the different roles of men and women, for instance. He also talks about the distinctiveness of both Jews and Gentiles.

The mystery of this "one new man" in Christ is not that Jews become Gentiles and Gentiles become Jews, any more than men become women or women men. The mystery is how two distinct peoples are now made into one community.

As a Jew, I find it curious coming across Gentile believers who want to become Jewish. So often these people seem to go over the top and risk being almost a caricature of what they think a Jewish person is like. Like converts to anything, they can become overzealous and turn everyone off the whole thing. When this happens, it is often a sign that that person has not fully found their identity in Christ and is therefore seeking something else. I find there can be a romanticization of the Jewish aspects of faith in these cases.

I'm not by any means talking about all people who feel called to identify with the Jewish people. Nonetheless, I have come across a sizeable minority who seem to get caught up in this exaggerated pursuit of a different identity.

In his letter to the Galatians, Paul was fierce toward the people he called "Judaizers." These people were demanding that Gentiles should become circumcised and follow the commandments of the Torah in the same manner as the Jews. Luke describes the context of this in the book of Acts:

> *While Paul and Barnabas were at Antioch of Syria, some men from Judea arrived and began to teach the believers: "Unless you are circumcised*

> *as required by the law of Moses, you cannot be saved." Paul and Barnabas disagreed with them, arguing vehemently. Finally, the church decided to send Paul and Barnabas to Jerusalem, accompanied by some local believers, to talk to the apostles and elders about this question* (Acts 15:1-2 NLT).

When they got to Jerusalem, a debate began:

> *When they arrived in Jerusalem, Barnabas and Paul were welcomed by the whole church, including the apostles and elders. They reported everything God had done through them. But then some of the believers who belonged to the sect of the Pharisees stood up and insisted, "The Gentile converts must be circumcised and required to follow the law of Moses." So the apostles and elders met together to resolve this issue* (Acts 15:4-6 NLT).

Peter reminded them of how God poured out the Holy Spirit on the Gentiles, and so "He confirmed that He accepts Gentiles by giving them the Holy Spirit, just as He did to us" (Acts 15:8 NLT). Then Paul and Barnabas weighed in by telling the others of the amazing things that had been happening among the Gentiles as they had been preaching the Gospel.

Finally, James outlined the apostles' and elders' conclusion. We looked at these verses earlier in a different context, but let's remind ourselves:

> *And so my judgment is that we should not make it difficult for the Gentiles who are turning to*

> *God. Instead, we should write and tell them to abstain from eating food offered to idols, from sexual immorality, from eating the meat of strangled animals, and from consuming blood. For these laws of Moses have been preached in Jewish synagogues in every city on every Sabbath for many generations* (Acts 15:19-21 NLT).

The apostles realized that if God wasn't requiring the Gentiles to convert or to follow all His commandments before accepting them, then neither should they. So, finally, they sent a letter to this effect, making the position clear to everyone—*Gentiles remain Gentiles as believers.*

Paul is therefore fierce with anyone who tries to overturn this principle, which is what we see in his letter to the Galatians. He wrote the letter specifically to address this error, which had been foisted on the believers there. When anyone tries to make Gentile believers feel they have to obey all the Torah commandments to the letter, and tries to tell the church it must do the same, they are trying to undo the edict that came from Jerusalem.

The apostles are doing something that Jesus told them they would do. He told them, "Whatever you bind on earth will be bound in heaven, and whatever you loose on earth will be loosed in heaven" (Matt. 16:19). This was a rabbinic phrase that related to interpreting Scripture, specifically God's commandments. Rabbis would determine for the people what things specifically were permitted or not according to particular commands. To "bind" simply meant to forbid, and to "loose" meant to allow. This was necessary because the commands give us umbrella statements (for example, "keep the Sabbath holy...do no ordinary work") but still leave us to define the details of what constitutes keeping them or not (E.g. Is driving on the Sabbath "ordinary work" or not?).

However, we must also see what the apostles are *not* saying. They do not say the Torah is no longer of relevance and thus unworthy of study by Gentiles. Part of the logic for not burdening the Gentiles is that the Jewish people have experienced centuries of teaching, whereas the Gentiles have no such background.

They are also not saying that Jewish people must abandon their practices based on the Torah. Quite the contrary—the whole need for this ruling could only have arisen if the Jewish believers were, as the disciples said to Paul, "zealous for the law (Torah)."

There is another principle that is also relevant here. Paul tells believers in Corinth to remain in the state they were in when they were saved. He's not talking about remaining in sin. Rather, he says if you're married, don't seek to be single suddenly, and so on. He says:

> *Each of you should continue to live in whatever situation the Lord has placed you, and remain as you were when God first called you. This is my rule for all the churches. For instance, a man who was circumcised before he became a believer should not try to reverse it. And the man who was uncircumcised when he became a believer should not be circumcised now* (1 Corinthians 7:17-18 NLT).

I have a book called *Are You Still Circumcised?* by Harold Rosen, a Jewish man. growing up in the East End of London in the 1930s. The title is a quote from a joke at the beginning of the book, and sums up the point nicely I think—you can't really undo circumcision![1]

Ultimately, the apostles and Paul were all in agreement—within their Messiah, Jews are to remain Jews, and Gentiles are to remain Gentiles. This is perfectly illustrated by Paul's analogy of the grafting process. When you graft a branch of a lemon tree onto an orange tree, it does not suddenly produce oranges but continues to produce lemons. It is simply drawing off the same source of nourishment as the orange branches.

We tend to skip over the judgment of the apostles too quickly. They instructed the new Gentile disciples to follow four key principles:

> *Therefore I judge that we should not trouble those from among the Gentiles who are turning to God, but that we write to them to abstain from things polluted by idols, from sexual immorality, from things strangled, and from blood* (Acts 15:19-20).

These are, in fact, also to be found in the book of Leviticus, chapters 17 and 18.

It's interesting that they make no reference to charity, to loving others, or to most of the things we might expect. They are not trying to sum up the Christian life. So why these four things?

There are different interpretations, but the most obvious seems to be this: they are both keeping Gentiles from maintaining pagan practices and facilitating fellowship between Jews and Gentiles.

God had already instructed the Jews not to do these four things nor to have fellowship with those who did. So if the Gentiles follow these four key principles, then keeping this new community together will be easier. Not simple, just easier!

Unfortunately, while the early church decided to let Gentiles remain Gentiles, as the centuries wore on the church began to insist that Jews must by no means remain Jews within the church. This is totally contrary to the thinking of Jesus and the apostles.

We perhaps see less explicit mentions made of the Jewish believers following a Jewish, biblical pattern of life, but we must be careful not to draw the wrong conclusions. This is not because they had abandoned their way of life and were going to church on Sunday, but because it was taken for granted that they lived as Jews.

We looked earlier at how, when the rumors were circulating that Paul had abandoned the Jewish laws and was teaching others to do the same, the apostles and Paul immediately took action. This passage in Acts 21 is absolutely vital to our understanding.

Luke tells us that he, Paul, and the others arrived in Jerusalem and went to meet with James and the elders of the church there. Paul explained the amazing things that God had been accomplishing among the Gentiles through him. Luke continues:

> *After hearing this, they praised God. And then they said, "You know, dear brother, how many*

> *thousands of Jews have also believed, and they all follow the law of Moses very seriously.* ***But the Jewish believers here in Jerusalem have been told that you are teaching all the Jews who live among the Gentiles to turn their backs on the laws of Moses. They've heard that you teach them not to circumcise their children or follow other Jewish customs.*** *What should we do? They will certainly hear that you have come.*
>
> *Here's what we want you to do. We have four men here who have completed their vow. Go with them to the Temple and join them in the purification ceremony, paying for them to have their heads ritually shaved.* ***Then everyone will know that the rumors are all false and that you yourself observe the Jewish laws.***
>
> *As for the Gentile believers, they should do what we already told them in a letter: They should abstain from eating food offered to idols, from consuming blood or the meat of strangled animals, and from sexual immorality."*
>
> ***So Paul went to the Temple the next day with the other men*** (Acts 21:20-26 NLT).

There could surely be no clearer illustration that Jews lived as Jews, even as believers!

First, there were countless followers of Jesus who were all Jewish and declared to be *zealous for the laws of Moses.* Then Paul, the person traditionally most associated with telling the church not to "go back to the law," went out of his way to publicly demonstrate that he lived as a Jew, and that any ideas that he had told Jewish people to abandon the Torah of Moses were false.

As we have seen, Paul's attempts to dispel these rumors were the catalyst for him going to prison and, ultimately, his death. Defending himself, he said:

> *Neither against the law of the Jews, nor against the temple, nor against Caesar have I offended in anything at all* (Acts 25:8).

And again:

> *And it came to pass after three days that Paul called the leaders of the Jews together. So when they had come together, he said to them: "Men and brethren, though I have done nothing against our people or the customs of our fathers, yet I was delivered as a prisoner from Jerusalem into the hands of the Romans"* (Acts 28:17).

Remember the prophecies of the prophets, of Jesus, and of Paul in Romans. They said there would come a time when the Jewish people—those branches broken off so the Gentiles could be grafted in—would be grafted back in and receive their true King.

We must ask ourselves—what this will look like? Does this mean that they will all become like Gentiles, except in name? Does it mean that a church in Tel Aviv will explode with Jewish people abandoning their Jewishness, Sabbath celebrations and their Passover holidays, celebrating Easter instead, and gleefully grilling bacon sandwiches on Saturdays?

Or is it about Jewish people seeing their Messiah as He truly is, finding Him right in the heart of their celebrations and their Torah, as He has always been, and as those early believers found Him?

When Jesus appeared to the two discouraged disciples on the road to Emmaus after His resurrection, it says He taught them all about Himself from the Scriptures—from what we call the "Old Testament."

It seems clear to me that Jewish people discovering their Messiah will need and want to remain as Jews. Actually, that is what we are beginning to see. I have had the privilege of speaking in Israel and the Ukraine to communities of believers who are living and flourishing as Jewish fellowships. They are finding a new path that is really an old path, as they themselves reconnect with the truth about Jesus, Israel, and the church.

In fact, in the process of Jewish believers coming to believe in Jesus as their Messiah, a number of fellowships (they would not call themselves churches) have sprung up across Israel, America, the UK, and many other countries around the world. They are based around a more Jewish model of Christianity—one that seeks to explore the ways those early Jewish believers would have lived out their faith in Jesus and to find a modern expression for this.

These communities usually call themselves "Messianic fellowships" or "Messianic synagogues." You may have heard of them. Some stick very closely to traditional Jewish practices, while some look closer to a modern church but with a Jewish flavor. These fellowships have begun to contribute much to the church in terms of what we are discussing, and they have helped many Jewish people get beyond the kinds of barriers we have looked at in considering Yeshua as their Messiah.

Sometimes they are misunderstood by all sides—rejected by their own natural brothers and sisters and also by the church, who see them as returning to legalism. Yet surely legalism is just when the outward form, the ritual, becomes the focus instead of the heart? And in my experience we can find legalism at different times and places in every individual, church community, and denomination.

I believe these new Messianic Jewish congregations are pioneering a path to creating fledgling communities—havens where the Jewish people will be able to find a true expression of their faith as they come to know their own King and Messiah.

This does not mean that every Jewish believer needs or wants to be in that kind of community. (I have been in a Pentecostal church since I have been a believer. I believe that God has set me there for a reason, although I also love, support, and connect with these Messianic Jewish congregations). Nor does it mean that these new fellowships are seeking to divide the body of Christ or rejecting other sections of it, any more than other new church communities are. If they adopt the principles of Paul that we have been looking at, they will embrace the whole body.

They are developing something fresh that can be a great blessing to us all as we look to restore the balance and to restore the lens of the Jewish context where it was lost. This in turn will help predominantly Gentile churches to embrace their heritage and become a welcoming environment for Jewish people who choose to make their spiritual home there.

ACTION

Try to find peace in who you are rather than seeking to adopt each other's identity. If you choose to follow customs and traditions from each other, don't let it be out of pressure or insecurity. Rather, find joy in them.

ENDNOTE

1. *Are You Still Circumcised? East End Memories*, Harold Rosen, 1999, Five Leaves Publications, Nottingham, UK.

CHAPTER 17

PRINCIPLE 4: UNITY

When I was quite a new believer, a very gifted and charismatic leader set up a Messianic Jewish fellowship in our city. He was an excellent teacher and a good man, and he began to build a community that was growing, based around a Jewish expression of the Gospel.

He would periodically say to me, "David, you're Jewish. What are you doing in a church? You belong in our fellowship!" Sometimes it was more flippant, sometimes more insistent, yet something didn't sit right with me about this.

It was not because I don't believe in this Jewish expression. As I said at the end of the last chapter, I do, and passionately. I believe it is a valuable and even vital journey for the church to make. I believe that this pattern that was lost needs to be rediscovered and pioneered for the benefit of all, with the principles I'm outlining here in mind. The many Jews who are coming to discover their Messiah need communities of faith whose expression has relevance to them and where they can develop an authentic biblical identity. The Gentile churches need to appreciate, encourage, and walk with them as they do this.

So in principle, when my friend said these things, I could see the logic and the attraction of what he was talking about. However, something felt wrong. There was a sense not only of difference but superiority that I detected in his attitude, and, fundamentally, there was a sense that all Jewish believers *must* be separate.

I had to push back and remind him that God had very supernaturally directed me to the church I was in. Therefore, I would need Him to equally supernaturally move me somewhere else. (Which, to this day, He never has.)

Sadly, this very gifted and charismatic leader ended up leading many people astray and moved into deception himself. The fellowship collapsed, at great cost to people's lives and the reputation of Messianic Judaism in the local area.

This is not God's way. As we have seen, Paul's concern in his letter to the Romans and elsewhere was that a sense of separation was occurring in the church—not only a physical or ceremonial separation, but a deep sense of disunity and mistrust.

Did this man's sense of isolation contribute to the tragic outcome? Would a closer relationship with the predominantly Gentile church have helped?

Paul previously stood up to Peter when he, as a Jewish leader, began to separate himself with other Jews from Gentile believers in the church in Antioch at mealtimes:

> *Now when Peter had come to Antioch, I withstood him to his face, because he was to be blamed; for before certain men came from James, he would eat with the Gentiles; but when they came, he withdrew and separated himself, fearing those who were of the circumcision. And the rest of the Jews also played the hypocrite with him, so that even Barnabas was carried away with their hypocrisy* (Galatians 2:11-13).

The issue was not just about following the Jewish dietary laws or not. Rather, it was about fellowship, and Paul challenged Peter over this idea of separation. His basic point was, "God has accepted the Gentile believers as part of His people; therefore, so must we. If God has poured out the same Spirit on them as us, who are we to separate ourselves from them?"

In Romans, Paul specifically addresses the other side of the coin. The Gentile believers in the church seem to have developed a sense that they have replaced the Jewish believers. They have become arrogant and are treating the Jewish believers as troublesome.

Paul reminds the Gentile believers that the Jews remain God's people, to whom they have been joined. He sums it up in this beautiful way toward the end of his letter:

> *Therefore, accept each other just as Christ has accepted you so that God will be given glory. Remember that Christ came as a servant to the Jews to show that God is true to the promises he made to their ancestors. He also came so that the*

> *Gentiles might give glory to God for his mercies to them* (Romans 15:7-9 NLT).

We Need One Another

Paul's final instructions and greetings are very interesting in this respect. First, he gives a long list of greetings to those in the Roman church whom he knows. Far more than in any other letter, he goes out of his way to name-check a whole range of Jews and Gentiles who are his friends. He identifies the Jews specifically as "my fellow Jews," so as to leave no one in any doubt.

He says things such as, "Give my greetings to Priscilla and Aquila, my co-workers in the ministry of Christ Jesus. In fact, they once risked their lives for me. I am thankful to them, and so are all the Gentile churches" (Rom. 16:3-4 NLT).

Paul does not list first Jews and then Gentiles, but very deliberately goes from one to the other and back again, acknowledging publicly his debt to both. In doing so, he perfectly illustrates for them this message he has been explaining for 16 long chapters—*we are better together. We need one another.*

Likewise Paul sends them greetings *from* a range of different people, again alternating between Jews and Gentiles. His final instruction is simple:

> *And now I make one more appeal, my dear brothers and sisters. Watch out for people who cause divisions and upset people's faith by teaching things contrary to what you have been taught* (Romans 16:17 NLT).

Paul urges them not to let anyone cause division in the community. He has spent the whole letter explaining how Jew and Gentile are one in Christ, distinct though they may be in many other ways. Now he explicitly urges them to remain in unity. Like a good sheepdog, he has gone from side to side to keep them together as they move forward, and now he urges them to remain as one flock.

In his letter to the Ephesians, Paul put it this way:

> *For He Himself is our peace, who has made both one, and has broken down the middle wall of separation* (Ephesians 2:14).

If this "middle wall of separation" has come down, we must stay unified and not build it again. This is a matter of both our hearts and our actions.

I have found that Gentile believers who discover the truths we have been discussing can sometimes become disdainful of the church. They disconnect with the communities they have been part of, or even the wider body, because they feel that this revelation is lacking. It is as if they can no longer see anything other than this one issue, forgetting all the good that the church is doing in so many other areas, and has often done for them.

But revelation from God's heart should always lead us to a *greater* love for His body on earth, the church. The principles contained in this book are not meant to bring a split in the church but a deeper revelation of who we are called to be. If the church is the bride of Christ, then she is Jew and Gentile *together*, and we must love her as she is. It's how we'll shine the brightest.

We have seen how reconnecting with the truth about the Jewish Jesus should lead us to a deeper revelation of who He is and a more intimate relationship with Him.

We have seen how reconnecting with the truth about Israel leads us to a deeper understanding of God's passion for His people, plus a greater awareness of His purposes being outworked today.

As we REWIRE our thinking and restore the Jewish lens regarding His church and allow these truths to come alive in us, it must also lead us to a more profound understanding of God's vision for the church.

I am Jewish and Denise is not. People have often asked us if Denise is going to convert and become a Jew. However, this doesn't seem to be our path. We are in marriage as a Jewish and a Gentile believer, together as one—both the mystery of marriage and of the church itself. We are fully united in Him, yet retain a certain distinctiveness that enhances who we are together as a family. We will teach our children to understand both aspects of their heritage. We will find a way to make this work as a source of blessing.

In the same way, the church is to be united, Jew and Gentile, together yet distinct, each valuing the other's heritage while sharing the same inheritance. Paul puts it this way:

> *Therefore, accept each other just as Christ has accepted you so that God will be given glory. Remember that Christ came as a servant to the Jews to show that God is true to the promises he made to their ancestors. He also came so that the Gentiles might give glory to God for his mercies to them* (Romans 15:7-9 NLT).

So we are together in Him, and, as in any marriage, the key to unity is to go beyond the platform of acceptance and learn to actually *serve* one another. This is the last principle that Paul emphasizes in his letter to the Romans.

ACTION

If you're in a Gentile church ask yourself this question: Would a Jewish person coming in feel welcome? Likewise, if you're in a Messianic Jewish fellowship, ask yourself: Would a Gentile coming in feel welcome?

CHAPTER 18

PRINCIPLE 5: SERVICE

We looked earlier at how the essence of Jesus' teaching in the Sermon on the Mount is to go beyond the minimum. Jesus tells His audience that it is not enough to avoid murder or theft. If you want to live righteously, then seek the very heart of God—to love others.

In the same way, Paul tells the Romans it is not enough to just *tolerate* one another as Jews and Gentiles. Love goes way beyond tolerance. There's a great expression—"Go where you're celebrated, not just tolerated!" Church should be a place where we don't just put up with but actively celebrate each other, walking together as one.

We can tolerate things and people that we think are somehow not quite what they should be. But Paul tells us this is not enough; we need to have a very different attitude toward one another as Jews and Gentiles. He says we must not elevate ourselves above one another, nor must we judge others for their form of observance. *We must go out of our way to actively prefer one another.*

We have seen how Jesus taught like the rabbis, who understood the concept of weighing heavier and lighter commands. The key to understanding Paul's instructions to the Romans is to understand this concept. Paul says:

> *Therefore let us not judge one another anymore, but rather resolve this, not to put a stumbling block or a cause to fall in our brother's way* (Romans 14:13).

He is not telling the Jews to abandon their practices nor the Gentiles to become Jews. He is saying that in all things the "heaviest" or most important command is to love one another. In the same way, Jesus reminded the Pharisees that although they were commanded to rest on the Sabbath, this principle didn't meant it wasn't right to heal or even to drag a donkey out of a ditch.

Our highest principle as we come together cannot be "Am I right?" but "Am I loving?" Paul said to Timothy, "The purpose [*telos*] of the commandment [*Torah*] is love from a pure heart" (1 Tim. 1:5).

In any marriage—or friendship, even—we soon discover this to be true. We can be "right" yet so wrong if our motivation is not love but pride or insecurity. As we mature and as we become more secure in our own identity, we learn to put the other person first in our decisions and plans. So as Jews and Gentiles, we must try to put each other first and not put stumbling blocks in each other's way.

When Jewish believers make Christians feel that their celebrations are invalid, they are putting a stumbling block there for Gentile believers, for if they celebrate the resurrection of Jesus by faith, this can only be a good thing. It is of no help for them to try and follow a legalistic pattern without faith.

Paul suggests that we go so far that "if another believer is distressed by what you eat, you are not acting in love if you eat it" (Rom. 14:15 NLT). As a footnote here, it is important to recognize that Paul is not referring to Jews eating kosher/non-kosher foods. Elsewhere, he has made clear that he never teaches the Jews to stop following the commandments of God, and this must include the dietary laws or else he is a liar.

He is actually talking about those who feel it is OK to eat meat versus those who eat only vegetables. That is clearly something among the believers that was causing controversy and offense, in addition to the issues between Jews and Gentiles, because no Jews were commanded anywhere to not eat meat. Moreover, Paul has said that his letter is primarily to the Gentiles. He warns us:

> *Why do you condemn another believer? Why do you look down on another believer? Remember, we will all stand before the judgment seat of God* (Romans 14:10 NLT).

At the beginning of his letter, Paul told the Gentile believers in Rome, his main audience, how much he was praying for them and how much he wanted to come and impart spiritual gifts to them. He had a profound desire to see them become fruitful.

> *For God is my witness, whom I serve with my spirit in the gospel of His Son, that without ceasing I make mention of you always in my prayers, making request if, by some means, now at last I may find a way in the will of God to come to you. For I long to see you, that I may impart to you some spiritual gift, so that you may be established—that is, that I may be encouraged together with you by the mutual faith both of you and me. Now I do not want you to be unaware, brethren, that I often planned to come to you (but was hindered until now), that I might have some fruit among you also, just as among the other Gentiles* (Romans 1:9-13).

Paul, a Jewish follower of this Jewish Jesus, is passionate about seeing the Gentiles become more fruitful. Even though he sees them rejecting the Jewish believers, his heart is still to love and serve them.

This must be our attitude too.

Again and again, Paul talks in the letters he writes about how he prays constantly for the different churches. The best way to serve one another is to allow God's love to grow in our hearts as we pray for one another.

There is also a sense of enlightened self-interest here, too. If the church is called to make the remaining Jews jealous, then the healthier and more flourishing it is, the more likely it is to impact the Jews who don't yet see Jesus as their Messiah. So for Jewish believers to serve the church is ultimately to serve the Jews, also.

And for the Gentile believers, if revival among the Jews is to be glorious, and "life from the dead," then it will bless all mankind. For them to serve the Jews is therefore to serve all.

Paul talks about how his heart breaks for his fellow Jews and how much he prays for them to come to know their Messiah. I believe God wants non-Jewish believers to carry that same heart and to pray for the Jews who don't yet know Him. The largest concentration of these is in Israel, but there is also the Diaspora—those spread across the nations of the earth.

Paul also highlights for the Romans how many Gentile believers, recognizing this debt they have, have been keen to bless the Jews materially.

> *But before I come, I must go to Jerusalem to take a gift to the believers there. For you see, the believers in Macedonia and Achaia have eagerly taken up an offering for the poor among the believers in Jerusalem.* ***They were glad to do this because they feel they owe a real debt to them. Since the Gentiles received the spiritual blessings of the Good News from the believers in Jerusalem, they feel the least they can do in return is to help them financially*** (Romans 15:25-27 NLT).

Paul doesn't explicitly tell them that they must do the same thing; however, he makes it clear that he sees it as a good and right thing. It fits perfectly with the thrust of the whole letter that we have been exploring. Jewish and

Gentile believers are called to appreciate, love, and bless one another, just as God has loved us.

This attitude is so far removed from where the church has been for most of its existence, but I believe God wants to bring us back to this place of serving one another. As in any good relationship, it is never a question of waiting for the other person to bless you but of stepping out unilaterally to do the will of God with a heart of love.

As we serve one another, we will see great blessings come to our lives and to our church communities, whatever they look like.

ACTION

Have an attitude of service toward one another. For Jewish believers, this means approaching the restoration of the Jewish lens with humility and a heart to see the church blessed. For Gentile believers, this means finding ways to bless the Jewish people, both those who are believers and those who are not. This can include showing your support for these new Messianic Jewish fellowships in Israel and elsewhere.

CONCLUSION

I am convinced that when the church applies these principles as Jewish and Gentile believers together, it will begin to shine more brightly in this world and see God move more powerfully than ever.

God gave us this mysterious marriage as two distinct peoples in just the same way as He gave man and woman marriage. Through this process He is developing His character and His heart in our lives.

This can only happen if we are willing to lay aside the traditions that cause us to see through a lens of half-truths and misconceptions and allow Him to reveal His heart and His glorious truths to us. We need to REWIRE our thinking by reconnecting with the truth about God's church.

The principles that Paul lays out for us as Jews and Gentiles are ones that the church has so often lost and then relearned—to walk with humility, not judging one another but serving one another; not trying to create uniformity of thinking and behavior, but an environment where each person can encounter their Savior and become all they are called to be.

The earliest manifestation of dysfunction is what Paul addresses in his letter to the Romans—in the marriage of Jewish and Gentile believers together. I believe, as we restore our understanding in these areas and learn to walk together, we will see the heart of God flow through our church communities like never before. He has given us to each other for this purpose.

We will see a healthier church that understands its debt to the Jewish people and how God's heart yearns to see them restored, not just physically to their land, but also spiritually to their Messiah.

We will see the great blessings that accompany God's promise to Abraham that "I will bless those who bless you" (Gen. 12:3).

The Jewish people will be more and more a part of this glorious kingdom that God is building in the hearts of men and women on the earth.

We can only see these things happening as we put the principles Paul outlines into practice. And we can only do that as we embrace the truths outlined in the first two parts of the book.

I hope that, as you have been reading, you have begun to understand the value of reconnecting with the truth about the Jewish Jesus. He is the original, authentic Jesus, from whom blessings flow for the benefit of all mankind.

I hope you have begun to feel God's heart for His people, Israel, and understand that He still has a purpose and a plan for them. As the followers of this Jewish King, it is a plan that we can all be part of. If God is truly doing something remarkable in the world with the Jewish people and the land itself, then we can choose to be a blessing to both.

I hope you can then go on and consider what God's true intention for the church is—this amazing community, this beautiful but flawed family composed of Jews and Gentiles working together to bring God's love to all nations.

This book may have raised as many questions as it has proposed answers. If so, I am glad. I pray that as you read the Bible and ask God to speak to you, He will REWIRE your thinking and bring alive these truths in a fresh way in your heart, so that you might restore the Jewish lens and know the Jewish Jesus more intimately, follow Him more closely, and allow Him to work through you more effectively.

Let me encourage you. As I said at the start, this is not a new layer to put on or a heavy burden to carry. Jesus said, "My yoke is easy and My burden is light" (Matt. 11:30). The yoke of a rabbi is his teaching, which is what Jesus was talking about—His *halakah*—His walk, or the way He encourages us to live out our faith.

So this is a liberation *into* the truth, as the layers come off and this Jewish Jesus begins to reveal His heart to us in a deeper, more profound way. Just like Joseph with his brothers in Egypt, we will all start to see Him more clearly and know Him more intimately.

I encourage you to read the Bible without the filters of tradition and to let God REWIRE your thinking. Put on the original, true lens—the perfect prescription of the

Jewish lens—and you will see how the new lines of detail emerge in glorious Technicolor!

I once heard a great Bible teacher called David Michael speak, and he said he wanted to give us the best key he knew to understanding the Bible. We were all waiting for some great intellectual nugget or technique. Instead he said just this: *slow down!*

So I pass on to you the same two words—*slow down*—because I believe they can revolutionize our thinking in this whole area. *Read Without Religion.* Stop and ask yourself what the text is really saying, especially those passages that seem unclear to you or difficult. Ask God how He wants to REWIRE your thinking. Let Him reveal the truth to you regarding the Jewish Jesus and His people Israel. Let him REWIRE your thinking about the church. Find other resources to help you understand all of this more. Pray for the Jewish people and get involved with blessing them and blessing the nation of Israel. I believe you will be amazed at how all of this enriches your faith and what God begins to do in your life!

About David Hoffbrand

DAVID HOFFBRAND grew up in a Jewish family in north London, and has a passion to see the church reconnect with the Jewish Jesus and the Jewish framework for understanding the Bible.

David and his wife Denise live in Brighton, England, with their son Isaac, where they are associate pastors at CityCoast Church, part of INC (international Network of Churches).

David has a BSc in Psychology and a Masters in Social Work. He previously worked as a social worker alongside various roles within the church.

David is also a singer-songwriter and has released three albums.

For further information and related resources please visit:

www.thejewishjesusbook.com

ACKNOWLEDGMENTS

This book owes as much to the input of others as it does to my own efforts, so I want to publically acknowledge and thank those who have helped along the way! Huge thanks therefore to:

My church family at CityCoast Church, Brighton, for providing a loving environment in which the understanding outlined in this book could flourish.

David and Jackie Harland for your unwavering support and encouragement throughout the years.

Ashley and Ruth Schmierer for your passion for Israel and encouragement to follow my dreams.

Adam Diment, my partner in crime, prayer, and Israeli food adventures.

My wonderful readers—Kaz Towner, Adam Diment, Jamie Harland, David Harland, & Denise Hoffbrand—for your endless patience in the face of seemingly endless edits (I will send you some more versions soon) and invaluable feedback!

My extra prayer support team—James and Jenny Meldrum, Simon and Lucinda Croft, & Rachel Wilson.

Danica Issell for your incredible, expert work in helping edit the manuscript and in some seriously detailed tweaking.

David Lee Martin for the timely advice!

Piers Arthur-Crowe for your friendship along the way, Ukranian adventures, and for encouraging me in the development of some of the themes in the book.

Igor Grishajev for wonderful yet mischievous facilitation of said Ukranian adventures.

Clive and Jane Urquhart for your friendship and support.

Jeff Lestz for really believing in the project and for introducing me to almost everyone in the world. You truly are 'a connector'!

Jurgen Matthesius for encouraging me in pursuing this and for providing a wide array of impersonations to accompany me along the way.

Brad and all at Destiny Image for your patience and flexibility as I worked and re-worked...and re-worked.

Barney (aka Ian Barnard) for designing a beautiful cover.

Finally, in writing this book I am absolutely standing on the shoulders of giants. I am indebted to the writings, study and speaking of so many on these subjects, but to list a few: Derek Prince, Lance Lambert, Dwight Pryor, Arnold Fruchtenbaum, Dan Juster, Michael Brown, David Bivin, Brad Young, Barry Horner, David Pawson, David Stern—these are just a few of the amazing authors who have aided my understanding and whose works I would thoroughly recommend for study and reflection.

LINKS TO CHARITABLE ORGANIZATIONS

If you want to find ways to support and bless both Jewish and non-Jewish inhabitants of Israel who are in need, as well as Jewish people around the world, here are links to some relevant organizations that I have connected with:

www.firm.org.il Fellowship of Israel Related Ministries (FIRM) is an umbrella organization working with a wide range of ministries that seek to bless Israel and the Jewish community around the world. This includes extensive engagement with and through the Messianic Jewish community.

www.visionforisrael.com Vision for Israel provides aid and assistance to the poor in Israel, regardless of ethnicity, through the Joseph Storehouse humanitarian aid centre.

www.israelrelief.org.il Israel Relief Aid provide aid to Israelis in need, regardless of ethnicity, and connect with a logistics network to facilitate the shipment of goods from other countries to Israel.

Also, a related organization that works to bring humanitarian aid to the wider region of the Middle East:

www.bringhope.info Bring Hope Humanitarian Foundation work primarily with refugees from the current crisis in Syria.

If you want to continue to develop a greater understanding of the subjects in the book, here are two organizations that might also be of interest:

www.thedavidhouse.org The David House is a UK based charity who do great work spreading an understanding of Jewish roots to the church and bringing together Jewish and Gentile believers. I am privileged to serve as a trustee.

www.jcstudies.com An amazing teaching resource that continues the legacy of Dwight A. Pryor